REAL ESTATE

&WEALTH

The New Edition

INVESTING
IN THE
AMERICAN
DREAM

by *Sonia Booker*

Foreword by Herman Russell

A complete source of information and
reference for investing in real estate

Plus 30 Wealth-Building Tips

A BEAUTIFUL MEDIA PUBLICATION

5652 Kingsport Drive, NE
Atlanta, GA 30342
404.847.0282
www.beautimedia.com

Book Design: Deborah Carson from Beautiful Media

Manufactured in the United State of America 987654321

Library of Congress Control Number: 3002111685

Booker, Sonia/Real Estate

The New Edition

ISBN: 9781499661088

www.SoniaBooker.com

This book is designed to provide accurate and authoritative information with regard to the subject matter covered. It is sold with the understanding that the author is not engaged in rendering legal, accounting, or other professional service. If legal advice or other expert assistance is required, the services of a competent professional should be sought.

Dedication

This book is dedicated to the thousands of people who I have met and heard from with my first book. I thank you for your support and your feedback regarding how the book helped you to build wealth. You inspired me to write a new edition that will continue to impact more lives. I am forever thankful that you allow me to share in your success!

Acknowledgments

My family is the most important thing in life and the best support system. You always support me, put up with me, and have helped me to adapt to some of my biggest changes in life. All of my family is truly wonderful, in particular my husband, Bernard, my son, Simon and my mother, Betty. I treasure you all.

A special thanks to my aunt Barbara, who was the first person to support my real estate endeavors, and for nurturing me to be a strong independent woman. My sister, Felicia who has worked with me for years, for her support and dedication, I carry you extremely close each day. My niece, DeAirah is a wondrous young lady with a gracious smile and faith; you are the best and my nephew, D.J. who reminds us all to follow our dreams.

My parents, grandparents and other family members at an early age, instilled my belief in myself. However, it has been Pastor Cynthia Hale of the Ray of Hope who has helped me to understand my ministry, and has nurtured my faith for over 15 years.

My team is the best, however I must single out Princella for your unwavering support of anything that I do, you are always there and Owen, you are priceless, I couldn't imagine the team without the magnitude of brilliance that you bring to the table. You are not only team members; you are good friends. Staci, and all of the members of Team Sonia, I tell you often how instrumental you are to the success of the vision, it's what happens behind the scenes that really matter. And the Inner Circle Women, just Wow, you inspire me more than I could ever inspire you!

And a special acknowledgment to Herman J. Russell, Sr. thank you for allowing me to sit at your feet, for all that you have taught me about entrepreneurship, real estate and just being an all around good person. You are the best mentor that anyone could ever have. I just hope that I am able to show you my gratitude by impacting the lives of others as you have done for me!

Foreword

Real estate is one of the most utilized investment tools today. It can entail something as simple as purchasing your first home. A home is generally a person's most valued asset, and in making this first purchase, an individual can be well on his or her way to personal growth and wealth. To truly begin to create wealth, an investor may begin purchasing real estate for resale and rental. In an age when investing in the stock market has proven to be risky, with lower margin returns and major losses, real estate has held steadfast and shown itself to be a great investment vehicle, especially for long term investors.

Sonia has given us a book to use as an instructional guide to getting started in real estate investment. It teaches the foundation of the activities one must undertake to succeed and get into the real estate game. Real estate is as fun as it is challenging, but the rewards of being a part of a successful deal and making a profit makes all the hard work worthwhile. An entrepreneurial spirit is key and self-motivation and good ethics play a role in sustained success.

In my lifetime, I have participated in many real estate transactions, and from my personal experience I can say that Real Estate & Wealth provides the tools of the industry that may take several years to learn on your own. Part of being successful in Real Estate is doing your homework. Become an expert in whatever sector or niche in which you choose to transact. Learn as much as you can and bring in the necessary support to fill in for your weaknesses. Relationships with well-educated professionals, such as appraisers, market analysts and mortgage brokers, are just as important as the knowledge the investor possesses.

Sonia discusses risk and how its levels affect the margin of return. This understanding is critical in growing your wealth. The more deals increase in complexity; the more profit an investor should expect to make. Another thought on this is the timing of returns. An investor can purchase at a relatively low cost in a declining or underdeveloped area, with the vision that at some time in the future it will grow. A vision is key, but one has to do the research and start to understand growth patterns and the life-cycle of neighborhoods.

Sonia has provided an essential manual on how to gain early success in real estate investment. The book should be taken and used as a "living-document"—take it and add your own pages of success.

Herman Russell

Table of Contents

Introduction

I first began investing in real estate about 15 years ago. Since that time I have bought and sold several properties primarily within the Atlanta metropolitan area. Now, more than ever, real estate has become a popular means of creating wealth, and this book was written as a tool and a reference guide for new investors. It was important for me to write a book that could be understood at any level. **REAL ESTATE AND WEALTH:** *Investing in the American Dream: The New Edition* accomplishes that and makes it easy for anyone to get started—now!

Making the choice *to be wealthy!*

It was once explained to me, very eloquently, that wealth starts from the inside and goes out. To be truly wealthy, you must possess characteristics such as integrity, honesty and sincerity, and with these elements as your base, you can begin to build your outside wealth. I believe this to be true. It was always important to me that, even though I was building my outside wealth, I was also building my inner wealth, and not compromising these traits of inner wealth in any situation. Let this guide you through your investment career, and you are bound to be a success.

REAL ESTATE AND WEALTH: *Investing in the American Dream: The New Edition* came to me one day as I was taking a personal inventory of my life and wealth. We all make choices in life, and being wealthy is a choice that we have to make. I decided at that point that I was going to make myself wealthy. Understand that everyone defines wealth and their goals differently; in my case, I meant that I was going to focus on activities that produced money, over which I could have more control. Having control of your money, taxes and investment decisions ultimately increase your chances of becoming wealthy. It was important to me to build wealth so that I could have a greater quality of life, retire early, travel and secure my future. It was also important to me to build wealth to have more choices in life: choices about how much money I had in the bank, in savings, where I could live, what I could drive, and the type of clothing I could afford to wear. Please understand, though, that I am by no means a materialistic person: I measure my wealth by assets and not things. The point is that if you want the "stuff," you can buy it, if you make the conscious choice.

My personal journey to becoming wealthy started with my quest to own real estate and to build profitable businesses. I understood one thing very well, and that was that I liked accumulating assets that built cash flow, equity that built net worth, residual income that built monthly cash flow, tax-free income and many other benefits that were needed, as I defined wealth. I soon came to realize that nothing comes without a high price, paid in time, commitment and dedication, but just like choosing to sacrifice myself for the betterment of my future, I simply chose to be wealthy. If you don't have the drive, the stamina, the guts, the endurance, the perseverance and self-encouragement to become wealthy, then this is not the book for you!

Making the choice *to invest in real estate!*

There are many investment vehicles, but I chose real estate because it is a tangible and understandable investment product. Many investments are on paper and you have very little, if any control over them. Investing in real estate offers more control and can lead to higher long-term growth.

Real estate investing is a flexible vehicle to creating wealth, whether as a hobby, to make extra money or as a full-time career. Many investors start out part-time with plans of progressing to full-time. Real estate investing allows for more family time and is accessible to both men and women of all ages.

This book deals solely with residential investing. The great thing about investing in residential real estate is the fact that everyone desires a place where family can have peace of mind, security and fellowship. In addition, there will always be a need for residential property!

Why is it important for me to share this information?

I once read that you can't lead someone further than you have gone, and believe me, I have gone a long way, and the unbelievable learning curve I have followed has led to my extensive amount of experience. Building a system and laying a solid foundation is something that I would like to share to see others become successful.

REAL ESTATE AND WEALTH: *Investing in the American Dream: The New Edition* shares stories of my personal investment experiences, as well as those of other investors. These experiences are shared in the hopes that, as a new investor, you can avoid costly mistakes, thereby increasing your success factor.

I hope that this book will confirm your view of real estate investing. It is important to gain a good understanding of how to invest correctly and profitably. Currently many people are investing and, unfortunately, they really never gained a good understanding of the process. Some have scored on a few deals, but inevitably I have seen that, without the proper guidance and foundation, they are not able to adjust when their luck runs out.

What I like most about this book

REAL ESTATE AND WEALTH: *Investing in the American Dream: The New Edition* presents a comprehensive and systematic approach to investing, including locating properties, obtaining financing, and selling or renting properties. As the author, I am most proud that this book can be used as reference and presents creative ideas to help you make quick cash and ease into a long-term wealth position. **REAL ESTATE AND WEALTH** encourages you to just get started, which is the most difficult part of investing. This book provides alternative solutions for new investors, such as "partnering" with another individual or a group. This type of investing offers support and a win-win situation for all parties involved, when done properly. "Partnering" makes room for busy schedules, so that all involved are able to share in profits, as well as the responsibilities that come with owning property.

Most importantly, this book makes it simple for anyone to begin investing and building wealth. The Appendix provides a *Real Estate Game Plan*, which will show you how investing in just one investment property can significantly build your net worth! That is exciting in itself, and, above all, it will show you how to create wealth for generations to come!

Happy investing...

NOTES

Chapter I

High Risk, High Reward!

The more you put at risk, the more you increase your chances for success.

I realize that not everyone can go around betting the farm, but you are about to take on some risk. You are the only person who can determine your risk tolerance. Don't base this decision on what anyone else is doing. There is such a thing as getting in over your head. So, if I can encourage you to do one thing, it would be to use this book as a guide when making your investment decisions.

Sometimes I laugh when I think that I owned ten pieces of real estate within three months of starting out! Knowing everything that I know now, it is not so funny. It is very possible, and I have worked with new investors who, learning from my information and the mistakes I made, have taken the same plunge and have reaped much higher rewards starting out, without the headaches.

If you are even considering real estate investing for building wealth or as a career opportunity, you are a pretty special person, because you certainly realize that there will be nothing average about it. However, you are finding out information and moving forward anyway. You are taking a risk!

Once you have read Chapter 3, you will begin to feel comfortable about the process of buying real estate. Knowledge builds your confidence, and by nature we are creatures who have a need for information.

Knowledge also builds courage, and with courage you are able to realize your true potential.

Above all, with each purchase the process becomes easier. Each time you purchase a property it is like giving birth. Your closing becomes the birth of the property: you nurture it, develop it, and finally it is all grown up. Once the property becomes self-sufficient, it is under control. In essence, when the property has a positive, healthy cash flow, it has developed properly, and very little maintenance is needed. Most importantly, you are able to move on to your next project—the next birth.

So what are you going to risk?

You should now be thinking very heavily about what you are willing to risk, and the reward(s) you are looking for in return. Everyone is looking to achieve a different reward, and that is why there is room for everyone in real estate investing. Your reward may be leaving your job, working as a full-time investor, or investing in real estate in order to raise money for college. Or maybe you just want to learn more about buying a home for yourself below market value.

My reward is introducing another person to the world of investing! It is so rewarding to think that I have learned a skill, which I can use to teach the rules of a game that a lot of people want to learn to play. Purchasing real estate is the biggest decision that most people will make in a lifetime, but you and I get to help with that decision, and as a result we are able to alter people's lives forever, simply by providing a nice home for them to live in. You will have the ability to make people's dreams come true, whether it is by renting a house, a lease-purchase or by selling them a home. You are able to affect someone else's life in a positive way, while helping yourself; that is the beauty of it!

Weigh your risk and make your individual decision based on the rewards you are looking to obtain, as well as your expectations about the business. Be honest and fair with yourself, knowing that you can always change your risk and rewards, depending on what is going on in your life. Setting unrealistic goals is not very healthy, and can be very frustrating. If you only have 5-10 ten hours a week to work at your investment goal, don't fool yourself into thinking that you will be able to squeeze in more. You will be disappointed every week, because you will feel that you have not accomplished your goals, and will eventually become discouraged by your perceived lack of effort.

Write down these two questions and think about the answers. Wait at least 24 hours, go back to the paper and review your answers to see if you still feel the same way.

What rewards are you expecting to gain from real estate investing?

Extra money, knowledge, wealth/asset accumulation, a career change?

What are you willing to risk for your reward? What must you risk to have the desired reward?

i.e. your free time, money, time with family, etc...

The answers to these questions will help you to begin formulating your personal real estate game plan. Your personal game plan will become your road map, and will set the pace for your real estate goals.

Real Estate Wealth Tip #1

To become wealthy in real estate, you must understand your risk tolerance.

Step 1: The Game Plan

It is imperative that you have a **game plan**. A copy of a suggested real estate game plan is located in the *Appendix* and can be used as a guide. A real estate investment game plan is just as important as your life plan. This plan will encourage you to stay on track with regard to your investment goals.

You will hear people refer to real estate as a "numbers" game. I will be the first to say that this is very true. The more properties you view and the more offers you make, the higher your chances of achieving your goals.

Note: So much has changed in the market, there is so much inventory on the market and it is moving very fast. The best way to compete is to narrow down your location and work that area hard. I will reference this point again with "niche investing".

Here I have made some adjustments in the thought process, mainly because I don't want you to become too aggressive. I would rather you focus on quality and not quantity. If you want to purchase two properties in a year, you will need to view at least 40-50 properties in a year's time to locate 4 or 5 that you will make offers on in order to get to your goal of 2. It takes a lot of work to locate a good deal, so you are going to have to exercise a lot of patience and make sure that you do your due diligence.

Writing your game plan will be more difficult than you think, and should reflect a commitment of your time, risks, and rewards. Just imagine your life now: it's pretty full already, and yet you are looking to commit even more of it. It is important not to underestimate your goals and what it will take to accomplish them.

Real Estate Wealth Tip #2

You become wealthy by being realistic and setting obtainable goals.

Step 2: Evaluating yourself

Take a few minutes to explore the following questions, which will further assist in formulating your investment game plan.

At this point in the process, I would strongly suggest that you order your personal credit report from all three reporting agencies. You can also start with www.freecreditreport.com then dive in for a closer look if your information appears to be off. You should also get into the habit of reviewing your personal credit report each year. See the *Appendix* for contact information.

---

1. How would you rate your financial position?

    ❏ Good ❏ Fair ❏ Poor

2. How would you rate your credit position?

    ❏ Good ❏ Fair ❏ Poor

How would you rate your financial position based on the amount of money you have saved or access to for purchasing an investment property?

*Note: For investors, you will need at least 20% down to have favorable loan terms. We will talk more about owner financing in Chapter 8.

Credit Rating Information

❏ A score of 579 or lower is considered a poor credit rating.

❏ A score of 580-619 is considered a fair credit rating.

❏ A score of 620-739 is considered a good credit rating.

❏ A score above 740 is an excellent credit rating.

3. How much money do you have readily available to invest?

4. How much money are you willing to invest?

5. Where will you get the money?—Savings, 401K, relative, paycheck, re-finance property, equity line?

6. Where will you get additional money if needed?

7. How much time will you be able to devote?

Before we go further, if you rated yourself fair or poor for any of above questions, or if you are not able to answer one of the questions, it is important that you address those concerns upfront. You may be in a situation where you have to use some of your money to take care of a few credit concerns before getting started. Or perhaps you should save up a little more money for your contingency or reserve.

Another alternative at this point, after evaluating your strengths and weaknesses, is to consider "partnering". There may be someone with whom you can partner who offers some of the things that you are lacking; this also makes for a good support system.

When choosing a partner, it is important to find out how the person can benefit the partnership. He or she doesn't necessarily have to bring experience; both people can decide to learn the process together and split the risk, as well as the profit. However, they should be complementary, and you should both understand each other's goals and objectives. My first investment property was done via a partnership, where I put up the down payment and financed the property and my partner did all of the renovations. This was ideal considering I was still running a business and he had the skillset and time to oversee the renovations. We sold the property and split the profits half and half.

Real Estate Wealth Tip #3

You become wealthy by creating a game plan that will guide your real estate investment path.

Step 3: Game Plan Matrix

You now have a good idea of how much time you have to devote to real estate investing, which will vary depending on your individual strategy.

You should also know how much money you have, and where you can get additional money if you need to. (More on this in "Financing Options," Chapter 8)

Credit Tips

First determine whether or not you are going to work with the bank or a mortgage company prior to granting authorization to research your credit. Don't be too eager during this process: interview them as well, but keep in mind that as you go from company to company requesting your credit history, this activity could eventually cause your credit rating to be lowered.

In this day of real estate investing, credit and money are equally as important. Gone are the days of having an outstanding credit profile and leaving the bank with a 90-95% investor loan. Or any loan for that matter. This is why I encourage you to have both.

People looking to invest their money in the real estate market and perhaps they have gone through a job transition or other financial hardships and their credit is not that great. Yet, in time they have managed to get on their feet and are able to make a substantial down payment of, say, $20,000–$30,000 on a $100,000 loan. You should be able to qualify for a good loan, meaning favorable interest rate and terms.

Note: You don't want to overpay for real estate based on your credit. In some cases it would be better to wait if there are minor issues. However, if you have major issues happening with your credit and you are still able to qualify for a loan, you may want to consider refinancing in a year or two. Most importantly just have a plan and don't overextend yourself.

As a first time homebuyer don't get boggled down on scores. Whether or not you'll qualify for a loan also depends on the reasons for the blemishes on your credit history and how long you have been back on the right track. It is understandable that situations occur; it is how you are able to overcome the situation that is weighed more heavily. I have seen people allow credit to become a negative factor, and it should not be. As a matter of fact, there should not be any factors to discourage you. Use this book to determine your best plan of action.

When you start to invest, your first goal should be to clean yourself up on paper. Your credit history should tell a story about your life, especially if it has blemishes: a responsible buyer should be able to explain them. Streamline your credit cards to fit your needs. Consider closing accounts that you have not used in a while, especially if they have a zero balance. Open credit accounts with zero balances tend to weigh down your credit score, and this is consequently viewed as a potential high debt situation. For example, at the time of your loan application you have two credit accounts open with zero balances but a combined available open-to-purchase amount of $40,000. Although the balance is zero at that time; the reality is that in a 24-hour period, basically overnight, you can accumulate $40,000 in debt! The risk involved with this can lower your credit rating. In the summary section of your credit report, a comment might appear, referencing "high available credit".

Note: Talk with a credit specialist; in some cases if you have had credit cards for a long period of time open, it could affect you negatively to close them. As with everything else, be intentional and strategic.

Another tip about your credit rating, is that once you have purchased a property, your rating may drop, so don't become alarmed. This sometimes happens because you now have what is considered "excessive new credit" or "credit too new to rate". It is seen as a negative at first, but once you have begun to make payments on time, for about six months, you will begin to see your rating starting to increase.

Once again I stress the importance of strengthening your credit rating especially prior to getting started in investing.

Real Estate Wealth Tip #4

You become wealthy by streamlining your consumer debt and cleaning up your credit report.

NOTES

_____

_____

_____

_____

_____

_____

_____

_____

_____

_____

CHAPTER 2

Getting Started

Understanding Real Estate Investing

"Are you ready for the challenge?"

Although you will be anxious to purchase your first property, don't be surprised if it takes a little time. Buying your first property can be compared to playing any type of sport: once you jump in and hit a home run, or shoot your first basket, it gets easier from there. Like any new venture, getting started is the hardest part.

I viewed hundreds of properties over a four-month period before finally deciding on my first purchase. Subsequently, the deal fell through at the closing table. The truth of the matter is that I was nervous and chickened out! I thought of a million reasons why I should not purchase the property, from the color to the size of the front porch. Basically, I am saying that it is okay to be apprehensive. From my first property to now, everything else has been a blur. I went from one house to twelve in my first year of investing.

As I look back on my decision to begin investing in real estate, I realize that it wasn't a very hard one to make. It was a field that I understood pretty well, from my family, spending summers working around a construction company paid off! . I will always remember my first solo major rehab project: it ran over budget, everything went wrong but it was a great experience regardless. Looking back on it and acknowledging the fact that I lost money on the front end of the deal, there was something exhilarating in seeing exactly what I had invested all of this money in! It was tangible; I could drive by any time and see my investment. That actually provided me some comfort,looking at those hard wood floors that I thought I wouldn't have to replace, I could see exactly where the extra $1000 bucks went. My strategy then became how could I make up the $1000 without compromising the look of the property; or how I could get more out of the sale to recoup the extra spending. Most other types of investments are on paper, and you don't have any control over them. Real estate investing is completely different; yes, there are some things that are uncontrollable, and yes, there is risk involved, but hands down it is one of the best investments that you can make!

Real estate is something that everyone understands, at least on the surface. You probably own a home now, or you rent a home, or you grew up in your parents' home. Either way you have a point of reference for real estate, which naturally puts your mind at ease.

You are able to make investment decisions based on things that make sense to all of us; such as:

- ✓ How fast is the neighborhood appreciating?
- ✓ What types of people are moving into the neighborhood; what type of person would move into this house?
- ✓ What repairs do I need to make to satisfy my investment criteria?
- ✓ Am I doing minimum work for the property to be a government rental?
- ✓ Am I doing work that requires a major rehab job to be attractive to a retail buyer?

Basic questions

When purchasing any property, ask yourself these two questions:

❑ What do I have to do to the property?

❑ What do I want to do to the property?

It is important that you are very clear about your plans for the property prior to making the purchase. You have to know the answers to these questions to gain a full understanding of the true cost associated with the investment.

An example of a need *and a* want...

I **need** to replace the roof on the property for functional ability.

I **want** to add a deck to the property for re-sell value purposes.

> **Real Estate Wealth Tip #5**
>
> *You become wealthy by being clear about your plans for the property prior to the purchase.*

Types of Investors

There are basically two types of investors and investment strategies.

1.   The Long-Term Investor (LTI)

This type of investor generally holds everything they purchase. He or she is systematic in how they operate and may use a management company to ensure that rent collection, repairs, management, etc... is in place. Property is purchased to accumulate long-term and generational wealth. This type of investor is looking for a good deal but understands that he or she may pay a little more for a sound investment and a property that doesn't need much work.

Buying-hold Investment Strategy:

Questions to ask when evaluating a good buy-hold property:

❑ Is the value consistently increasing?

❑ How stable is the neighborhood?

❑ What is the condition of the property?

❑ Are there a lot of homes for sale within the area?

❑ Does there appear to be a lot of undesirable activity being carried out in the area?

❑ Are positive changes taking place in the neighborhood? Do you see signs of revitalization?

❑ Is the neighborhood diversifying; are higher income classes of people moving into the area?

❑ Who will manage the property?

❑ Do you understand the rental market? Not understanding your rental market and how to locate tenants fast can single-handedly wipe out any potential profits. Making payments on a property longer than planned is not a good thing.

Real Estate Wealth Tip #6

To become wealthy you must understand the market.

When purchasing for long-term purposes, it is important to be informed and involved. You may want to sit in on neighborhood and community meetings to get some insight. Call your local city agencies to find out information on when and where these meetings take place. A hands-on approach goes a long way when you are trying to gain knowledge about a particular area.

2. The Short-Term Investor (STI)

This type of investor generally purchases property for a quick re-sell in order to generate cash. The holding time is 90 days or less depending on the amount of repairs could go up to six months. Keep in mind that this type of investor can also pick up a property and sell it to another investor for quick cash. This type of investor generally doesn't have the time to invest long-term, or only has one goal at the time: to build cash.

Buy-Sell Investment Strategy

Why do you want to sell?

Answering this question leads you to the determining factor of whether you should buy-hold or buy-sell.

The buy-hold strategy is covered first, because it is more involved than buy-sell. There are additional factors that must be considered.

❑ Do I want the responsibility of tenants?

❑ Do I have a reserve for unforeseen factors that may come up with the property?

❑ Is my cash flow able to support my other investment plans?

❑ Keep in mind that you should have both short-term and long-term investment goals and strategies. You could very well start out using the buy-sell strategy, then build up to the buy-hold strategy. Buy-hold is a long-term goal, while buy-sell builds quick cash flow.

❑ Your financing options can be quite different depending on which decision you make. (Financing options are discussed in more detail in Chapter 8).

Partnering

When you are starting out, look for properties that need very little work. I would not advise jumping into a major renovation job at first: there can be many drawbacks to doing that. (Additional information on this appears in Chapter 5—"Rehabs"). I recommend, if possible, working with an experienced investor from whom you can learn. However, if two new investors are both committed and dedicated to learning the process, it is not necessary for either party to have experience. Partnering can be highly effective for your first couple of deals. Once you learn the ropes and adjust to your market, you can graduate to investing solo.

There are several ways of forming a "partnering" relationship:

1) One investor is responsible for obtaining the loan on the property; the experienced investor is responsible for teaching the other investor the ropes. Once the property is renovated and sold through joint effort, the partners can split the profit 60/40, 50/50, 70/30, or whatever is mutually agreed upon.

2) One investor could obtain a loan for the property. The other investor would pay for the repairs and, once the property is sold, profits are split 50/50.

Be sure to enter into some form of written contract, specifying the terms and expectations, as well as what defines the end of the relationship. (See *Appendix* for *Partnering Contracts*)

Group Partnering

Another concept to practice is "group partnering." This can include investment clubs or parties with more than two people.

"Group Partnering" can also include a group of investors coming together to purchase a property in cash. Say that the property is $60,000 and requires $20,000 in rehab work. The After Repair Value (ARV) for the property is $125,000. If four people invest $20,000 each, potential earnings would be $45,000 or $11,250 each, they should be able to turn this property within 120-180 days. Not a bad investment, considering there are no holding costs associated with the transaction. Even if you added some selling cost 3-5%, you would still turn a pretty decent profit.

"Group Partnering" is also good for purchasing multi-family units; as long as defined arrangements are in place and it benefits all parties involved.

Drawbacks to "partnering"

In most cases, you will have to sell or refinance the property to close the transaction. If you are going to hold the property, make sure that the numbers work for at least an 80% re-finance (See example).

I don't recommend holding property jointly with other investors. Partnering is more popular on a short-term-defined basis, unless experience has shown that you can safely handle long-term investments together.

Note: If you are partnering with a family member or good friend it may work to keep the long-term investment. Just remember that there has to be some specified future plan for the property(s).

Other drawbacks

❑ Each of the partners may have conflicting agendas with regard to the property.

❑ There may not be a real cut-off or end to the investment transaction.

❑ Splitting up is often an encumbering process, usually done by liquidating property and dividing the proceeds.

However, I have seen investors partner in different types of transactions with the same person, deal after deal. The point is that they have found a way to create a good balance and leverage each other.

Real Estate Wealth Tip #7

You can become wealthy in real estate by practicing the concept of "partnering."

Quick Calculation

Initial Loan

Purchase Price	$80,000
	$64,000
	{New Investor Loan}
	$16,000
	{New Investor Down Payment}
Repairs	$10,000
	{Experienced}
TOTAL INVESTMENT	$90,000
*ARV	$150,000

Refinance

80% of ARV	$120,000
Repay Debt	$90,000
Profit	$30,000
New Investor	$15,000
	{In addition to the asset}
Experienced	$15,000

Based on a 50/50 partnership

*ARV-After Repair Value

If you decide to keep the property, you will also have to factor rental payments into this calculation, so that you are able to make enough to cover your mortgage payments, including taxes and insurance. As a new investor, I can't think of any reason why you would want to run a negative monthly cash flow.

Refinance transaction

Let's say that you refinance at a 6% interest rate. Your payments on $120,000 will be approximately $700.00, not including taxes and insurance. Say that taxes in the area for the previous year were $1000.00, and insurance premiums were $400.00. This would increase your monthly payment by ($1,400/12) $116.67, thus bringing the total monthly payment to roughly $820.00.

In researching the rents in the area, you determine that you can get $1,000 in rental income. Having your down payment back, an asset with $30,000 in equity (ARV of $150,000 less loan balance of $120,000), and $180.00 in monthly cash flow, that wouldn't be a bad deal. Now you can take your original investment and repeat this process!

The flip side is that you are not able to get as much rent in the area. You would want to consider cashing out less, lowering your cash profit, but raising your owner's equity. Keep in mind that the other investor's profit is what you are trying to cover—this amount is $15,000 (based on a 50/50 partnership).

What will the number have to be if you can only get $900.00 in rental payments?

You could lower the loan amount to $105,000, in order to pay off the initial investment of $90,000 to obtain a more manageable mortgage payment. This way, you have $15,000 to use in paying off the other investor. Your mortgage payments, with taxes and insurance, will be around $750.00, giving you a net rental cash flow of $150.00.

Sell the property

If you sell the property at the ARV of $150,000 and pay off the original debt of $90,000, the available profit is $60,000. You are probably thinking, "why would you not sell the property to double your profit?" Let's say that the house is located in an area that is experiencing double-digit appreciation 10%, for example. If you sold the property today, you will make $60,000, but in just 12 additional months the property will be worth $165,000, thus leaving $15,000 to be made in additional profit. Or maybe you do not need the cash, and you would rather allow the property to continue appreciating.

As stated earlier, you must have a clear plan as to what you are going to do with the property prior to entering into the arrangement. If you change in mid-stream and try to convince the other investor that he or she should be happy with $15,000 in a buy/hold plan, when he or she clearly set out to make $30,000 from a sell, this conversation will not go very well.

The biggest secret to "partnering" is that it must be a win-win transaction for both parties involved. Make the deal attractive to another investor; make it worth his time to invest with you. If you are not sure how to structure a partnering transaction, ask an experienced investor to propose a deal, and see if it is something that you can live with. Remember that you will only have to do this a couple of times before you get the hang of it.

NOTES

CHAPTER 3

Go Slow—Research, Research, Research

How To Determine If It's A Good Deal

If you are like me, you are ready to jump in the water head first, of course—only later figuring out the proper strokes and techniques, but realizing that it is never too late to learn how to swim.

This chapter will take you through an in-depth research phase. You will see why it is important to practice what I call "niche investing". This term refers to locating a market with which you will become extremely familiar. This means that you should know when something in this area is sold, when something is rented, and when something is new on the market. In due time you will become more sophisticated and able to work two or three markets, but for now, just concentrate on one. Once you learn how to research, you will be able to buy property anywhere!

Another important reason for "niche-investing" is that the locations of your properties will be fairly centralized. This is important, especially for rental property.

Market Research

Important professionals to know:

❑ Mortgage Broker or Bank

❑ Certified Real Estate Appraiser

❑ Licensed Real Estate Agent

❑ Licensed Contractor

A word of caution when working with these professionals: keep in mind that they specialize. Look for one's who deal primarily with investment properties. He or she will be a much better resource and will save you a ton of grief.

Your process will start with a mortgage broker or banker. Knowing where your money supply will come from is pretty important. Most new investors make the mistake of finding a property first without knowing where and how they will finance it.

Understanding Your Financing Options

Mortgage Broker/Banker

Immediately start building a good professional support team. Since you will rely heavily upon your mortgage broker or banker, make sure that he or she understands both your short-term goals, as well as your long-term ones.

This professional should be fairly accessible, have experience in working with investors and be familiar with financing options and recommendations. If you don't get the feeling that his/her knowledge level is there, it is probably not necessary to go further into the process.

Important questions to ask:

- ❑ What is his or her background in working with investors?
- ❑ What types of programs are available for investors?
- ❑ What amount and what percent of the loan will you qualify for?
- ❑ How will you need to structure your investment deals?
- ❑ How much money will you need for a down payment and closing costs?
- ❑ How much money will you need upfront?

These are all very important questions; however, they are designed only to establish information about the knowledge level of the professional. *(Financing options are covered thoroughly in Chapter 8).*

Believe me, you don't want to work with an inexperienced mortgage professional, especially not when you are starting out. This inexperience can be very costly!

An experienced broker/banker who works with investors will know exactly how to package each individual investor.

He/she should be able to make recommendations as to how to create the most favorable investment strategy.

This person will also be able to provide you with your credit rating, and make suggestions as to whether or not you will be able to raise the score prior to getting started.

Understanding the Value of the Area

The Real Estate Appraiser

During the real estate downturn, it was deemed that the market value had drastically increased and some areas had inflated values. Now, to keep this from happening again the banks are regulating the appraisers more by randomly choosing from a pool appraiser's as opposed to the investor or agent having the appraisal done.

The real estate appraiser remains a highly important part of the research process. This professional holds a state-issued license and, in essence, determines the value of the property through an in-depth research process known as "comparable analysis". Through this process, the appraiser is able to compare like properties to the subject property. It is customary to determine the "true market price" through locating two or three similar properties and making adjustments for square footage and other factors that determines value.

For a property to be chosen as a comparable, it had to be sold within the last twelve months. This comparable analysis report also allows you to compare the subject property by square footage, construction type, date built, number of bedrooms/bathrooms and whether there are any additional amenities, such as a basement, porch, deck, pool, and so on, which would enhance the value of the property. The result of this information should provide you with a good indication of how much you should purchase the property for, as well as what the property can be sold for.

It's a good idea to talk to the appraiser on a regular basis. He/she is a good source of market information, during your research phase, until you have become familiar with the area. Ask the appraiser to provide you with comparable information for a particular address or area that you may be interested in investing in.

If the appraiser is not familiar with the area, it is even more important for you to take this list and go for drive. At this point you should be noting, very carefully, the properties that are listed on this report. *Has the home been renovated? Does it look realistic for the area? Don't compare a house in bad condition with a house that has been fully renovated, unless you are looking to purchase the property, renovate and retail it.* This will give you a good indication of the after-repair value (ARV) of the property. Basically, you want to be sure that you are comparing apples to apples.

If the appraiser is familiar with the area, he or she should be able to readily give you information about the property, as well as the surrounding area. I personally work with some good appraisers, and from working with them and performing "niche investing", they are very familiar with the areas in which I invest. Whenever I call them, they are a wealth of information!

Note: With the increase of the Internet since this book was first written, several online resources are easily available such as Zillow and Trulia. I use these all of the time, yet when I really want to know something, nothing beats that one-one-one perspective and information.

When you first start there may be a slight fee involved for receiving information, depending on the appraiser. However, once you establish yourself as a "serious" investor, it becomes much easier to obtain information and is usually free. Also check with your local Real Estate Investors Association (known as REIA). In most states, these organizations usually allow you to use various programs on-site and online and this service is included in your annual membership fee. It is also good to be members of organizations which allow you to meet and interact with other investors. Notice, I didn't say do business necessarily.

(How to review an appraisal is located in the *Appendix*).

Understanding the sales in the area

The Real Estate Agent

Locating property through real estate agents is becoming increasingly popular, due to the high amount of foreclosed properties. Banks are finding it to their advantage to list the property for maximum payoffs.

Locate a licensed real estate agent to work with, one who is experienced in working with investors. Allow me to caution you that this will be a very challenging process. Most agents do not care to work with investors, mainly because it is a lot of work! Fortunately for me, I have developed some good relationships with agents over the years; however, it was not always that way. Again, as you establish yourself as a "serious" investor, this process will become easier as well. Ask other investors for the names of their agent(s).

The key is to establish a good, mutually beneficial working relationship. You will find that most investors do not use real estate agents at all, mainly because they feel that they cut into their profits. Personally I agree, but I will show you when they can be useful and how to work with them effectively. Agents claim that they spend a lot of time with investors who never purchase anything or list anything; if this were true, you could see how this would become frustrating for agents.

I have gone through my share of agents, eventually parting ways due to their lack of urgency. When you become very serious and passionate about investing, you quickly understand that time is money. It is important that you work with professionals who share the same or a similar sense of urgency, or the relationship is not going to work.

The time frame that it takes for you to get information is essential. Sometimes, while I am out driving through a neighborhood that I am not familiar, I call my agent for information on the spot, or I am at least able to have the information within an hour, while the area is still fresh in my mind. A good agent understands the urgent need for information when making an investment decision.

The Multiple Listing Service (MLS) can be used at your local REIA, if you are a member to look up properties yourself. Once again, these services usually come free of charge with membership, so find out what resources are available to you. However, your ultimate objective is to build a team of professionals who have a common goal in financing, locating and appraising your property. Allow each to work within their respective areas. Also remember they are compensated for their services, so don't let any of them make you feel like you owe them a favor. If you are keeping them busy, they should not mind doing a little upfront legwork for you. If they do mind, they are not the team players you are looking for!

Another tool to become familiar is the Comparative Market Analysis (CMA). This report is prepared by a real estate agent and provides you with information such as the average sales price and average days the property has been on the market. See the *Appendix* for a sample CMA report. Again, Trulia and Zillow are excellent forums and convenient to use.

Real estate agents are also very good for listing your properties; a good relationship is created when they know that they will do all or at least the majority of your listings. This type of relationship makes them feel as though their efforts have not been in vain, thereby forming an understanding that the legwork is all part of the deal. All of this is important to know when you are going to be investing in a particular area.

Once you have this information, go through it and then ask the agent questions, such as:

❑ Why are the houses staying on the market for so long? (If over 70 days).

❑ Why are houses selling lower than the list price? (If selling consistently for more than 20% under list price.)

❑ Why are houses selling over the listed price?

Usually, when you see property sales being raised above the listing price on a consistent basis, it signifies a strong buying area. Buyers are literally in bidding wars for the property, thus driving up the value. Unless there is some type of sentimental reason involved, the seller will usually take the highest offer on the property. This is also a good indication of a potentially "hot" area, especially if there are not a lot of houses for sale in the area.

Look carefully at the sales to determine whether or not individuals/ families are moving into the area. You should drive by, especially on the weekends and evenings, to see what types of people are out in the neighborhood. This is to make sure that your area is not infested with bad sales; this could affect your investment decision. Once again, if the agent is not familiar with this area, you will need to go out and look at the addresses on the report. At this point you are looking for potential problems in the area by analyzing the validity of the reports to the best of your ability with the assistance of a trusted sales agent.

Real Estate Wealth Tip #8

A sure way to become wealthy in real estate is by gathering a good team of industry professionals.

Don't Make Assumptions

You should be very observant and realistic about the properties on the list. Don't assume that the only reason the house sold under-market or stayed on the market for an extended period of time is because someone did not do a quality renovation job. Maybe it was listed too high for the market, or the appraisal could not support the value. Maybe the area is becoming less desirable, and the houses in the area are actually depreciating. Or maybe the owners just wanted a fast sell after a divorce. The point is that you never know, and that is why you have to *research, research, research!!*

Real Estate Wealth Tip #9

In order to become wealthy it is imperative that you understand how to perform market research.

While you are out in the field, viewing your "comps" report and analyzing the CMA, once again, talk to the neighbors: they are an excellent source of information.

Your research is imperative for knowing whether or not you are making a good investment. There is nothing worse than making a purchase and later finding out that you paid too much! Is that not our worst fear? Once you get the hang of this process and develop a team of professionals, it will go a lot smoother. If you begin practicing the technique of "niche investing" that I suggested, your battle is halfway over. You will never feel like you have all of the answers; however, look at the numbers and avoid making emotional decisions, as they can cost you.

While you are in the field, keep in mind that it does not matter whether or not you would live in the property. That said, I would never recommend an investor to purchase property in areas that he or she doesn't feel comfortable in. The point is to research the area and let the numbers determine whether or not it is a good investment.

Real Estate Wealth Tip #10

You can become wealthy by practicing the concept of "niche-investing."

Real Estate Agents for Listings

I know investors who haggle over listing fees; I, on the other hand, don't get into that. I like to see everyone around me make money. As an investor, I don't feel that I should be the only one profiting from a good deal. Yes, I think that I should make more money from the transaction, but that is because I am taking all of the risk and inheriting all of the future responsibilities associated with owning the property. An agent who works with you on a regular basis should be rewarded. Besides, by-owner selling is very time-consuming, and can take away from more productive investment activities. Just add the fee for their service into your sales price. (More about selling your own properties in Chapter 7.)

The research process will become easier once you have gone through it a few times. "Niche investing" is an individual approach to "area investing". You should start to learn an area inside out; niche/area investing also helps you to create an impact. When you create an impact, you have more control over the area in which you are investing. When partaking in "area investing," these investors target areas in which everyone actively purchases property, knowing that by practicing this concept, they are able to have a profitable impact, thus helping all of their investing efforts.

I practice this concept with other investors and have been able to make major impacts within certain areas. It also forces you to become involved in other neighborhood efforts. I have served on the Board of Directors for a park within a community in which I invest heavily. I know that people moving into certain areas expect green space and recreational involvement; parks are what provide a balance in a community, not to mention that they are an important factor when considering property value increases.

You should also get into the habit of talking to the neighbors about selling their properties; the object is to have as many properties in one area as possible.

If they are not interested in selling, have your contractor talk to them about completing some minor improvements. Sometimes you can work with your contractor to gain more work in a particular area, and with this accomplishment, they will be able to do the work for a discounted price. This is attractive to most contractors because they are able to stay busy in one area and don't have to go looking for more work. (More in "Rehabs," Chapter 5)

As you can see, there are many suggested requirements for being a successful investor. Community involvement, effective research, team building...and you haven't even bought your first property yet! However, once you are part of a partnership or a group investment relationship, a lot of the responsibility and risk can be divided.

Real Estate Wealth Tip #11

To become wealthy, you should practice the concept of area investing. Locate an area within which to create an impact, and watch the value increase.

NOTES

CHAPTER 4

Locating Property

Where To Locate The Deal Of A Lifetime

"Good deals are often created, not located. You should always be looking for a good investment deal. Opportunity is all around you!"

There are several ways of locating properties. In this chapter I will discuss effective ways of implementing strategies that will bring you good deals. The ultimate idea of property location is to have the property find you. Bird dogs, contract assignments, pre-foreclosures, foreclosures, farming, for sale by owner (FSBO), lease-purchases, newspapers, and the Multiple Listing Service (MLS) are all examples of effective ways to locate properties.

Talking with other investors, and from my own experience, I have found that a combination of methods is most effective. My motto has always been "nothing happens until you locate a good deal." I believe this to be the single most important phase of the investing process. Locating the property is an art, and every deal is completely different.

I refer to the process as an art, because you should approach each deal creatively. The art is to create ways that you can purchase a property with as little out-of-pocket as possible. Using a lot of your own money out of necessity is okay, but it can slow you down because you are only able to buy so much.

Note: When you are using your own money, always have a clear picture of how and when to expect it back.

The Art of the Deal

The true art is to make a deal work for both you and the seller. Don't take this part of the learning process for granted; understanding various structuring techniques will save you a lot of money. Locating properties and creating good deals is all in the structuring. As long as you have a motivated seller, the sky is the limit. When talking with any seller it is important to identify their needs. Find a solution that will satisfy your goals, as well as the needs of the seller, and everyone will be happy. Yes, it is just that simple!

Most sellers only understand traditional means of selling their property. It is your responsibility to educate and show them that there are other profitable methods, especially at times when the market is slow. There can be considerable advantages for the seller in not selling by traditional means. Outright sells can come with major tax implications and cash flow concerns. When you educate them, you win as well.

Real Estate Wealth Tip #12

To become wealthy you must understand that the best investment deals are the ones that you create!

Once you get started, you will find other methods and enhance different systems to fit your market and the type of properties that you are looking for. Real estate investors are all different; each has a target market and strategy. Just remember: don't re-create the wheel!

With any system, you must have discipline and dedication. Whatever your strategy, remain consistent and remember that most systems take time to get up and running.

Bird-dogs

A method with which I have been very successful is a process known as using bird-dogs. I have noticed that they have renamed themselves as Property Consultants. With this method you pay for leads only if you purchase the property. Put your feelers out and let people know what type of properties and areas you are looking for. I am surprised when a day goes by and I do not receive at least one lead on a potential deal.

Check with a real estate attorney in your area about the legalities involved with paying bird-dogs. In some states it is tricky because you are only able to pay licensed real estate agents for locating property. So check it out and figure out how to make it work legally. The seller pays this fee from his/her sales proceeds; it doesn't come directly form you. Bird-dogs can be as involved or uninvolved as you would like for them to be. Because this is the person who establishes the groundwork and makes the first contact, it is not a bad idea to allow them to handle the transaction under your direction. Or if you prefer, at the point when the price and terms are being agreed upon, you can take over the transaction then.

I personally prefer to keep bird-dogs in the field, where they are most productive; I usually become involved in the process fairly early. Remember, bird-dogs are not paid until you actually close on the property, so you can't have too many.

Some bird-dogs advertise in local newspapers to get telephone calls from distressed sellers. Understand that good bird-dogs can make a full-time job out of just locating properties for investors. This is a quick way of earning cash with very little overhead or start-up cost. This process requires no credit or cash! The biggest challenge is to have qualified investors who are ready to purchase.

Pre-Foreclosures

This is another of my favorite methods of locating properties. Just like all the other methods, it has become increasingly competitive. Pre-foreclosure information is usually public record: anyone is privileged to it. This information must be posted in a local newspaper and ran for a certain number of days, by law in most states. The key to this strategy is to be creative in your approach. The owner should feel something from you, some sense of desire, loyalty, and sincerity. At this stage, owners are still very emotional about the potential loss of their property; they are looking for a buyer who they feel will take care of the property. There is definitely no magical method however, when I am dealing with pre-foreclosure sellers, my approach is to provide fast and realistic options. I am very honest and forthcoming about what I can and can't do. I educate them about their options and their lack of time, and then I back off. My callback rate is pretty high with this helpful approach.

Various Approaches

- ❏ I know some investors who use the "end of the world" approach or high-pressure techniques.
- ❏ There is no right or wrong approach; I encourage you to find a way to reach this group.
- ❏ I also use a combination of door hangers and mailings, as well as face-to-face interaction.

Financing considerations when working with pre-foreclosures

Consider your cash flow and your means of obtaining quick financing. There are basically two ways to stop a foreclosure. One, you can pay the arrears to the foreclosing attorney. Two, you can purchase the property outright from the owner for the mortgage balance, plus any additional fees and, of course, interest.

The arrears can be anywhere from $2,000 to $20,000, depending on the situation and the amount of the monthly mortgage payments. Once you have paid the arrears, the loan is brought current, and you then begin making the regular monthly payments to the mortgage company under a land contract with the owner and take possession of the property. This process is also referred to as a "subject-to" contract;

the rights can also be transferred using a quit-claim deed. (Consult with your real estate attorney regarding the best method). Basically you are taking over the existing lien and terms. This transfer of property rights is done by using a warranty deed or a quit-claim deed. In this day of real estate investing, I would advise that once you secure the property by way of deed; quickly move into finding a financing option to secure the property. This way you avoid some major issues with the loan remaining in the seller's name and the lender calling the loan due, which could put you in a bind if you are not financial prepared. More importantly, it puts your cash investment at risk. (See the *Appendix* for a sample Quit-Claim Deed)

This transfer of title should be handled through an attorney's office to ensure that it does not come back to bite you. Keep in mind that had they sold the property earlier on the retail market, they would have probably made something from the sale. Point being, you want to be fair but remember you are not there to save their lives but there to save their property.

Caution:

Prior to proceeding with the transaction to purchase the pre-foreclosed property, be sure to have a title search done. This is done to determine what liens or other encroachments exist that may hinder you in being able to gain clear title to the property. There is a fee for this service; you can also go to the courthouse yourself to locate information about the title. (Some counties are behind in updating their records, so you could possibly miss something that a professional title examiner will be able to locate). In addition, titles that are searched through a professional examiner are warranted and guaranteed.

This process may seem very cumbersome, especially when you are trying to move quickly on a property, but they can save you a lot of money and grief later on!

When making back-payments, it is important to have a quit-claim deed signed and notarized for the specified amount prior to making the back-payments. Having the deed to the property signed protects you from the owner attempting to sell the property from under you. Your recording will show up on the title. Once again, consult with a real estate attorney on whether or not to file it immediately, depending on how you are planning to handle the financing. In most counties you can pay extra to have a rush filing done, which will show up on title a lot faster.

Caution:

With so many people getting into real estate investing now, the title search becomes an absolute must to ensure that the person you are contracting with is the person who has the right to sell the property. Believe it or not, there are many contracts and earnest deposits paid to sellers who have no rights to a property. They will take several contracts and deposits on one property without actually being able sell it to anyone. Needless to say, it is impossible to locate them once you have paid and later find out that they cannot actually sell the property. Unfortunately, they are counting on you not performing a title search.

Foreclosures

I have only gone to the courthouse steps once in my investing career. I am not a big advocate of purchasing from the courthouse steps and it is somewhat now reserved for what I consider the major players. They are purchasing 10-20 properties at a time, which makes it hard for an individual investor to leverage this process. If you are the type of investor looking for a few properties a year or may one or two in your lifetime, there are more viable options out there for you. The other issue for a small investor is that you purchase from the courthouse steps, you are purchasing site unseen. Which means that you are inherited a property that you have no idea of the condition of the inside. Yes, this could spell disaster. Believe it or not I have heard and seen situations where owners trash houses due to being upset about the loss of the property.

The foreclosure process varies from state to state or county to county.

It is important to learn how the process works in your area and determine whether it will be a viable option for you. For instance, in some states the foreclosure process is daily instead of monthly, which means that at any given time you can walk up to the courthouse and get a good deal. In other states there is a wonderful foreclosure process, which makes it easy and hassle free to purchase because the old title is wiped completely clean at the time of the new purchase.

Drawbacks/The unknowns...

❏ The title may not be clear and you can't purchase title insurance, therefore risking a lot of unknown.

❏ You are purchasing sight unseen. I have seen property owners literally destroy the house because they are losing it. You are probably familiar with the area, but when you have not seen the interior you have no idea what repairs, and so on, might be needed.

❏ This is a serious game and I have seen many investors lose their shirts at it.

❏ You must have immediate availability to certified funds to purchase from the courthouse steps.

Keep in mind, when handling these types of transactions, that time is of the essence: the faster you move, the better. If you do choose this method, "partnering" would not be a bad idea. Locate an investor who has experience in this type of investing to show you the ropes.

Real Estate Wealth Tip #13

To become wealthy you must understand that discipline and dedication are both strong virtues in investing.

Contract Assignments

Once you get the hang of various types of transactions, you can go out negotiate and assign contracts to other investors. This process can be involved and tricky, so be sure you know what you are doing. When you have obtained the rights to assign a contract, it should be written in your name and, legally, you must have some means of purchasing the property if you are not successful with assigning it. Be sure to add specified language to the contract, stating the time frame, assignment clause and amount of the fee to be paid. This fee is usually paid from the seller's proceeds to you for locating a buyer.

I have seen assignment fees of anywhere from $500-$5,000, depending on the property and the equity margin. You have done most of the legwork as an assignor, but once you pass the property to another investor, the majority of the responsibility is theirs, so don't get greedy! An average fee is around $1,000-$2,500, depending on the time involved. The fee is usually less than an agent's listing fee and it is considered a finder's fee, since you are not licensed.

Another key to making this process work smoothly is to have qualified investors who are able to purchase fast. When I am assigning a contract I always know to whom I am going to assign a contract at the time of negotiations.

This contract with the owner should be structured with maximum protection, as well as "a get-out clause" in case you have trouble assigning it. Don't string the contract out: if you are unable to assign it within 72 hours or less, drop it; you are now holding up the property for no good reason. In addition, it is not fair to the owner!

In most states it is perfectly fine to add this fee to the closing statement, and you are paid directly by the attorney at the time of closing. Most contract assignments are done by investors, unlike bird-dogs. Contract assignments become popular when your system of locating good deals allows you to find more than you can purchase yourself. By using contract assignments for the overflow, it keeps your process in place and when you reach your monthly goal, assign the rest of the contracts to other investors.

Sample Clause

"Seller is aware that this is an assignable contract. I have 72 hours to have it assigned or my contract is terminated. If I assign the contract within 72 hours, my fee for locating a buyer is $2,500, payable at time of closing."

Real Estate Wealth Tip #14

To become wealthy you should always perform a title search prior to drawing up the final contract on any property.

Farming

Farming can be very effective, but time and follow-up are absolutely critical! If time is something you don't have, I definitely don't recommend this process. Basically, farming involves launching a mailing campaign, targeting your niche-investment area. Postcards and street signs work well and are not very expensive. (There are sample postcards in the *Appendix*).

If you don't have much money when starting out, but you are willing to devote your time, this is an excellent method. You only need paper, postage and a car to begin farming. A 24-hour voice recording is good to have, but not a necessity. When you are farming, the idea is that you are looking for a motivated seller. Make sure that you are targeting the seller of the property, and not a tenant. There are several ways of finding out who owns the property; the most effective is through the use of tax records.

The concept of farming supports "niche-investing." It can also be carried out in conjunction with other methods of locating property.

You should already have identified an area of opportunity through your market research. There are several ways of obtaining street addresses; however, the best way, when starting out, is to go for a drive and jot down the sequence of the streets, then mail 4-5 streets a week and follow up by telephone with as many owners as you can. This exercise will familiarize you with the area even further.

Other ways of obtaining street addresses, as well as owner names, are:

❑ Obtaining tax records from the courthouse. Many counties make this information available on-line. Real estate agents are also able to provide this information.

❑ Now with the use of Google maps and other online map services, you can easily obtain all sorts of information.

Remember that repetition is important. You want the person to receive mail from you at least once a month, and perhaps in the sixth month, you will catch them at a time when they are ready to sell. Yes, it can happen, but being systematic will increase your chances.

I have found that owners are moved by certain events in their life, and you never know what might provoke a sale:

❑ Retirement
❑ Job loss
❑ Divorce
❑ Children leaving for college
❑ Relocating
❑ Moving
❑ Debt relief

For Sale By Owner (FSBO)

This is an excellent source for obtaining good deals, as well as for locating lease-purchase opportunities. A lot of these properties are offered under market value; real estate agents have not coached them, or they have priced their property for a quick sell. Some are not aware of trends or increasing values in the area.

When dealing with FSBO's, you are definitely looking for motivation. If the seller is not motivated, it is difficult to structure a good deal.

Research your tax records carefully with this group. It is important to know what they owe, in relation to what they are asking. The tax record information also provides you with square footage, age, lot size and other pertinent information, which can assist in the bargaining process. For the most part, this group believes that listing the property with a Realtor and paying 5-7% of their profit is a rip-off. Some can't afford to pay an agent and still cover the mortgage balance and manage to make any type of profit.

Example:

The mortgage balance is $89,000, purchased four years ago for $92,000. The current market price is only $95,000; a 6% commission is $5,700, leaving a balance of $89,300. No closing costs have been paid. This means that the seller will make $300, or, worse, will have to pay some closing cost to get the house sold and have to pay the difference to sell their property from their own pocket.

You can turn this into a great deal by offering a lease-purchase!

The transaction would then look something like this:

Offer to pay the owner $1,000 down and $800 a month (the mortgage payments are $700). The $1,000 is more than they would have made by selling the property. Locate a buyer for the property with $2,000 down and $1,000 a month. For structuring this deal to work for everyone, your reward is $1,000 upfront and $200 a month. Not a bad deal, considering no money was paid out of pocket.

This type of scenario works well when the rental market is up and people are paying higher rents. Also, in a cases where people are looking to move in order to purchase a larger house while the interest rates and inventory is favorable but don't have any options for their existing property.

Lease-Purchase

There is an entire chapter devoted to this process because it is unique and deserves special attention.

Online Newspapers

Newspapers are a good source for locating motivated sellers. The For Sale By Owner section as well as the For Rent section are the headings to search under. Many owners who advertise in the rental section may actually be interested in selling the property. Maybe the property has been on the market too long, and they just need to get someone into the property to cover the monthly debt. It doesn't hurt to talk with this group about both lease-purchase and quick sales. The newspaper is also good for learning more about an area, as well as getting to know other investors who are advertising. You will also find that a lot of investors use the newspaper to advertise lease-purchases; they are looking for buyers, but you may be able to make some of these transactions work in your favor.

Finally, newspaper advertisements can give you a good indication of the average selling prices for both non-renovated and renovated properties. You will also get a good idea of what is going on in the rental market.

Overall the online and paper newspapers are a good source of information.

Multiple Listings Service (MLS)

There are times when MLS is a good tool for locating investment properties. There are a couple of points to remember when using this process: make the offers <u>attractive</u> and <u>fast</u>. This method is also very competitive, more of a "rat race", and this is why you will need to have a system in place that will allow you to identify these properties fast, and have financing in place to be able to close on them equally as fast. Think about it this way: if you own a property that requires you to make monthly payments, you have one factor working against you, which is that every month the property is on the market, you have to make monthly payments. Say that based on the market averages for time on market, if you are in a hot area, people will probably come looking to purchase your property prior to you putting it on the market. On the other hand, if you are not in such a "hot" area, then you are taking a gamble. The reality is that if the payments on the property are $900 per month, in 90 days of market time you will have paid out roughly $3,000. If you have the opportunity to sell the property within the first 30 days, you will be able to make up some of your projected out-of-pocket expenses. The challenging part is finding an agent who can present this thought process to the seller.

Say that you locate a property through the use of MLS. You make an offer $10,000 below the asking price. Within the offer, you make note that the property is being purchased "as is", with a closing date of 10-14 days from acceptance. Holding the property on the market for 6 months can cost them $5,400 of their potential profit! Prices are normally listed higher in this category, anyway, to be able to include the sales commission. So there is usually leverage when using this process.

When to use MLS/FMLS...

The use of these services are very effective in areas that have higher-than-average appreciation margins. If you are able to obtain the property for just a little under market value and don't have to put much work into it, you are basically holding/renting it as the value is increasing. Having investing vision is important in order to be able to see where an area is progressing.

Some areas and types of property are not ideal for buying through the use of MLS. However, with the increased bank inventory they have began listing their foreclosed properties through agents for maximum exposure.

Real Estate Wealth Tip #15

To become wealthy in real estate you must be able to recognize what is motivating the seller.

Real Estate Wealth Tip #16

To become wealthy using MLS the key is to make attractive offers that can be closed fast.

What to look for...

Types of listings

❑ Newly listed properties that have just gone onto the market.

Making an offer on a newly listed house can be a good thing to a motivated seller. They may not like your offer very much, but they like the fact that you can close quickly on the transaction and that they are able to move on faster.

❑ Houses over 90 days become market-sensitive.

These owners are usually very motivated, because they anticipated that they would sell the property within 90 days. They also realize that the longer they are left holding the property, the more costly it becomes for them.

Re-listings

❑ Agents write listing contracts with time periods anywhere from 90-120 days.

If the property does not sell within that time frame, some owners allow the agent to re-list the property, or have it re-listed through another agency. A re-listing is also motivating for the agent to sell because everyone involved is somewhat anxious to put the property to rest.

Vacancies

❑ If you can locate a property that is vacant and has a mortgage balance, you will normally find a motivated seller.

Combine the vacancy with over 90 days and it becomes even more motivating. Property that does not have a mortgage balance is a good target because the owner is still responsible for the upkeep of the property, and might also be concerned about vandalism and theft to the property.

Vacant property creates anxiety due to safety issues, as well as the burden of a double mortgage, in some cases. Houses that have been vacant for an extended period of time are also good potential lease-purchase deals. Once again, if you have a good agent who can negotiate this transaction, you will be better off. Depending on the type of contract the seller has with the agency, you can try to pursue the purchase directly with the owner once the listing has expired.

Undervalued houses

It is definitely a good idea to know your market; otherwise you will not be able to recognize when property is being offered under market value.

Agents are able to provide you with "hot sheets." This list contains information about all of the new listings in a particular area, with prices shown in descending order. It is also a good idea to receive this on a daily basis so that you can be one of the first people to go out and view the new listings. If this is one of your processes, it is vital that your agent contacts you with this information on a daily or fairly regular basis, preferably by fax or email.

> **Real Estate Wealth Tip #17**
>
> *To become wealthy using MLS, you must be able to view the property immediately and be prepared to make an offer.*

Writing Contracts

Once again, you need an investment-savvy agent who will make sure that the contract is written with at least one "get out" clause. This is extremely important when writing any contract, because sometimes it buys you time to get more answers. Once you are able to have certain information confirmed, you may not feel the same about purchasing the property. Maybe the appraised value wasn't high enough for your investment criteria, or maybe a better deal came along.

Nonetheless, don't tie up the property for more than 48–72 hours from the acceptance date. Just think: if it were your property, you would not like someone preventing you from selling it to another buyer. Furthermore, you don't create any animosity if you handle this in a timely manner and you are able to receive any earnest money back and salvage a working relationship. (There is a sample contract in the *Appendix*.)

Some of good "get out" clauses:

❏ Purchase is based on buyer's contractor inspecting the property within 72 hours.

❏ Purchase is based on inspection being performed at the buyer's expense within 72 hours. (If you do not have a contractor.)

❏ Purchase is based on the appraised value being at least 10% higher than the asking price.

❏ Purchase is based on buyer's attorney approval of the property within 5 days.

❏ With regard to a lease-purchase, the contract should state that it is based on you being able to locate a tenant-buyer within 30 days, or a specified time.

Real Estate Wealth Tip #18

To become wealthy in real estate you must understand how to use "get out" clauses.

Caution:

Never state that a licensed inspector will do the inspection: this way you will only have to produce a write-up from your contractor, etc, and not have to pay for a full inspection report. Basically, you are stating that the property requires more work than you thought.

Believe it or not, you are now ready to go out and talk to sellers, through newspapers, bird-dogs and FSBO's, and create some good deals! How to analyze whether or not you have located a good deal:

Review Transaction:

As you can see, there are certain controlled variables:

❏ If you were able to have quality repairs done for less than $5,000, that would create additional profit.

❏ If you are able to make fewer mortgage payments, i.e. two, that would increase your bottom line by $500.00.

❏ If you were able to sell the property yourself through newspaper advertising, out-front signage, word-of-mouth, and so on, this would increase your profit by over $4,250 or ½ of commission fee!

However, be realistic: some investors would gladly take the $8,250 profit, because they simply don't have the time to spend taking calls and showing the property. If you have time, especially when you first start out, you may seriously want to consider selling the property yourself to maximize your profits. Bottom line, this done correctly, could make you $8,250 to $10,000+ in three months or less, not bad.

Tip:

Always figure these numbers higher than you expect them to be. This would be considered a worst-case analysis.

NOTES

CHAPTER 5

Rehabs

How To Rehab Effectively

"When to rehab and when to run!"

Rehab is a short form of the word "rehabilitate," which means to fix or to make whole again. This is a term that you will hear often within the real estate investment industry. To make a property whole again is to "rehab" the property. Rehabbing, in my opinion, is different from repairing, in the sense that a repair can be thought of as something minor. I can repair the leak in the sink, or I can have someone patch the ceiling. However, a rehab is a major undertaking, a more elaborate process.

Most investors either take on rehab projects, or they do not consider doing rehabs at all. Investors like myself will consider rehab projects at the right time and in the right circumstances. My absolute minimum profit that I will consider making from undertaking a major rehab job is $30,000. This margin is set because my holding time can be much longer. If I must hold a property for six months while carrying out a rehab job, I figure I should make at least $5,000 per month; otherwise, it is better for me to stick to a 45-90 day turnaround project. By having a faster turnaround I am able to move through more properties.

It is not always to your advantage to undertake a rehab project. There are several factors to consider when making this decision: low cash flow; not enough reserve; you don't have a good subcontractor to do the work at the time; or you may have too many rehab jobs going on at one time. I am stressing the importance of making the best decision—whether to rehab or to run—because of the high costs associated when your rehab projects are not analyzed accurately. This is one of the biggest ways new investors lose money!

Maybe you picked up a property at a good deal, but for one or more of the reasons mentioned, it is not feasible for you to do the rehab job yourself. That is the beauty and flexibility of real estate investing. At this point you could pass the property, by means of contract assignment, to another investor, or you could look for a partner who is in a better position to help with the rehab project, or sell the property to another investor. Remember to look for ways that you can still benefit from locating the deal. Once again, it is important to enter into a circle with other investors, so that passing the property becomes smooth and quick.

Types of Rehabs:

Major rehabs

Major rehab jobs typically cost over $10K. Most major components will have to be replaced, and the job will typically run from 90-180 days. Usually all major components are replaced during this process. Major components include HVAC (heating ventilation and air-condition unit), plumbing, electrical, and roofing. Also, note that you will need to make sure that the contractors working on the first three components hold a state-issued license. This is very important when it comes to inspection codes and permitting (depending on your county's requirements).

Because there can be so many unforeseen factors when approaching a major rehab, think in terms of worst-case scenario when determining your time-frame and budget. What is the absolute highest price it can cost for this rehab job, plus a Rehabs 20% reserve? If, when the 20%

is added to the cost, profits are lowered considerably, you may want to consider passing on the project. There are too many headaches associated with the job to not make any profit! This is the only way you can make a rational decision, especially until you get the hang of doing these types of jobs.

Consider whether or not to undertake a major rehab by calculating the monthly payments (referred to as holding costs) required while the renovation is underway. For example, if monthly payments on the loan are $600.00. Over six months, holding cost would be $3,600. As you can see, this number can be significant, and is based upon the interest rate that you are able to obtain.

The investors who make the most amount of profit with major rehabs are the ones who do their own work. These investors are able use their time and knowledge rather than their money. Remember that the highest cost associated with rehab is labor. In most cases labor is at least 75% of the total cost. However, most investors have neither the skill nor the time to do the work themselves.

I have seen it work very well in these cases when an investor partners with a contractor. By making this person your partner, he or she has a vested interest in completing the work on schedule and within the budget. In addition, you don't have to spend time overseeing the contractor.

Major rehabs are not recommended for new investors. There is so much to learn, and that is why I advise gradually building up to this point.

Real Estate Wealth Tip #19

To become wealthy is to understand when using a partner can be your benefit. Be willing to sacrifice profit for knowledge.

Minor rehabs

Minor rehab jobs are typically under $10K and can usually be completed within 30 days. Only one if any major component is replaced. For the most part, only cosmetic (paint, carpet and minor enhancements) work is performed.

The advanced new investor can handle this type of rehab. It is also worthwhile taking on a partner for beginning rehab jobs. Once again, you will be able to learn the ropes, as well as some short cuts, which can save you a lot of money.

Look for a good development company to work with; this can facilitate your rehab project. Most development companies have lower overhead than general contractors. Shop around to find a good, reputable and trustworthy company. When investing, it is imperative to keep your repairs within your budget. This even applies to the smallest detail related to the rehab job.

As you approach each rehab job, bear in mind what you can do to the property that will make it stand out. If you don't feel like you will be able to make an impact on the outer appearance of the property, you may want to consider whether or not you want to take on the project. This is important especially if you are going to sell the property. You must be able to convince everyone else that there have been big changes made to the property, and that it does deserve the price that you are requesting. Remember that when you are renovating property, you want to create "curb appeal": this is what draws someone to the inside of the property. I have seen investors do a super quality job to the interior of the property, but from the outer appearance you would never have guessed it! Lack of curb appeal also increases your market time.

Landscape, paint colors and exterior lighting are all ways of creating curb appeal for a property.

Real Estate Wealth Tip #20

To become wealthy you must be creative in making "curb appeal." Understand the improvements that will add value and the improvements that do not add value to the property.

What to watch for when rehabbing:

Rehabbing is very challenging. Most investors quit after their first major rehab project, because they have lost money and come to feel that investing is not for them. Some new investors do not even complete the project!

Obtaining rehab quotes is similar to taking your car into the shop for repairs: we feel that no one has our best interest at heart, and that we are being given incorrect information, because we really don't know. This is why you must learn the basics of rehabbing so that you know enough to know both when you are being taking advantage of and when you are getting a reasonable deal. Experience will be your best teacher, but knowledge will make it more bearable.

I am extremely apprehensive about touching on what you should expect to pay, because all regions are different. Rehabs in the south are typically less expensive than rehabs in the north, but there are always exceptions to the rule. With this in mind, I will stick more to methodology and provide you with a format that you will be able to tailor to make sure that you don't miss anything when figuring your cost. You should become an expert at knowing what to look for, so that you will be able to make quick assessments about a potential investment.

Recommendations

Experienced Investors

Once again consider partnering with an experienced rehab investor; follow the investor around while he or she is figuring cost and getting bids. This should become second nature. Also, ask around for referrals from other investors, or, if you see a crew working on another property, stop by and view their work. You can also get an idea of this process by using some of the following methods:

Telephone Estimates

Use a mock house and call from the telephone book, asking subcontractors or vendors the same questions. Have two or three painters provide you with an estimate to paint interior walls: good condition, no patching required, all white, 2 rooms 11X14, and 1-room 10X10, ceilings included. Some quote by square footage and others quote by number of rooms. This will be an interesting exercise.

Repeat the process, calling other contractors. Request them to provide you with an estimate for replacing a roof of 400 square feet; replacing decking; and removing two layers of shingles. You must be able to calculate your square footage in order to obtain accurate quotes. (Measure the length of the area and the width of the area, then multiply the two numbers to figure the total square footage).

Note: Get two quotes for this: one with you supplying material and one for the cost when they provide material. This exercise will allow you to become familiar with the language of contractors.

PRO Books

You can purchase books to show you how to do almost anything. Home Depot and Lowe's provide free copies of their PRO Book. You can also obtain a copy from almost any builder's supply store. PRO Books are excellent guides and references for figuring material cost. However, you should definitely have a PRO Book from the store from which you purchase the majority of your supplies. Again, with the Internet, so much of this can be done right online.

When carrying out "replacement rehabs", add a 25% factor to the standard price to install. For example, if you are replacing the HVAC system, on top of the standard cost of the unit, factor in an additional 25% to account for the labor to remove and discard the old unit. If the price for installing the new unit is $2,000, figure another $200 to remove the old. This can vary, but is a good rule of thumb.

Contingencies

An example of the need for a contingency would be if your budget included refinishing the hardwood floors throughout the property. Later in the job it is discovered that the floors are weak and soft in the living room. Instead of refinishing them you must replace the floor in that room, including the sub-flooring underneath. You had only budgeted for $200 for that one room and $1,200 for the entire job; now that one room alone will cost $1,000—an additional $800, increasing your total to $2,000! I can give you countless examples of where this happens, because some things are just unforeseen. This is why you need to set aside contingency funds.

There is a sample cost estimate form in the *Appendix*. You should fine-tune your own based on the prices that you are able to obtain for certain work. For instance, I am able to get some things done cheaper because of frequency and workload. Always negotiate a discount based on these factors, and it is also important to remind the contractor of your loyalty and that there are other contractors that you can call.

Real Estate Wealth Tip #21

To become wealthy it is imperative that you gain a solid understanding of rehabs.

Contractors vs. Sub-contractors

I prefer working directly with sub-contractors. However, it takes a while to become familiar with their work. I look for sub-contractors who take pride in what they do. The main purpose of the contractor is to oversee the sub-contractors and keep the job moving on schedule. The contractor will build in a fee of anywhere from 10-25%. However, if you are just starting out, the markup is probably worth it until you learn the ropes yourself.

Keep in mind that coordinating subcontractors and checking on job activities at the property is a very time-consuming process. Development companies and contractors have more access and time to do this.

How to pay contractors

Many contractors don't have an operating budget that allows for him or her to pay for materials prior to starting the job. The most effective method is for you to purchase the materials and have them delivered to the job or picked up by the contractor. Avoid paying a down payment for labor. Always pay according to stages of the job, to ensure that the work is finished before all the money is paid. This is a huge mistake that new investors make. They are so anxious to have the work done that rationale goes out the window.

I have known investors (including myself) who paid contractors 25% or 50% down, and they never showed up to do any work. I have also seen contractors inflate the cost of materials, adding an astronomical markup to the overall costs. The only way that you can maintain your cost is to know how much you should expect to pay for labor and other associated costs.

Real Estate Wealth Tip #22

To become wealthy you must understand how to manage contractors.

Material cost and Labor cost

Become very clear about estimating materials and labor; and be reasonable when dealing with materials and your time. Many investors try to micro-manage this process, to the point that they end up losing a lot of time picking up and delivering materials. As mentioned you can also have the materials delivered to the job site, for a small fee; just make sure that someone is there to take delivery.

Pay your contractor/sub-contractor on an as-work-completed basis, meaning that once the work has been completed and inspected, they are paid according to contract.

Most sub-contractors operate on an immediate gratification system. Once they have completed the work, the sooner you pay them, the better. You are more likely to get a quicker response from them on future jobs, and they generally get your work done pretty efficiently, so that they can get paid and move on to the next job. Sub-contractors certainly understand that time is money.

Writing contracts

When writing a contract for your contractor and sub-contractors, I recommend that you use a contract like the one located in the *Appendix*: it includes hold-harmless agreements and waivers that are to your benefit as an investor. You should have the contractor sign a lien waiver, if possible, for maximum protection.

You should also hold contractors accountable for their work. By creating an accountability system, you are forcing them to look at the job thoroughly, instead of bidding low to get the contract. If they are held responsible for a percentage of the total job for going over budget, they will be less likely to do so and more likely to give you a more accurate estimate. Another tip is to charge your contractor a daily rate for each day he or she goes over the agreed-upon time limit for the job. Based on the time frame stated in the contract, this amount can be based on what you will lose daily if the property is not rented. This can be based on the daily interest amount associated with the loan, or a flat daily fee. This should definitely be written into the contract, with the penalties spelled out. If your contractor or sub-contractor does not want to sign the contract based on this clause, it probably means that he or she was not planning to finish within the time frame stated in the bid. This clause should be within reason and should take into account things such as inclement weather and other mishaps out of the control of the contractor. For example, the contract should allow at least 7-10 days over the agreed-upon completion date, and penalties should begin to accumulate only after that window has expired.

Other Tips:

- ❑ Get referrals and/or references
- ❑ Always add a contingency of at least 10-15% on all jobs (higher for houses older than 1970 and on major rehabs).
- ❑ Hold contractors firmly to their estimates.
- ❑ Build in a bonus to ensure that estimates stay under budget by involving your contractor or sub-contractors.
- ❑ Consider "partnering" with a contractor to control your costs and increase profitability.
- ❑ Use specialty sub-contractors in their designated fields; if his or her field is painting, don't allow that sub-contractor to do the plumbing, to save money. It will end up costing you in the long run.

NOTES

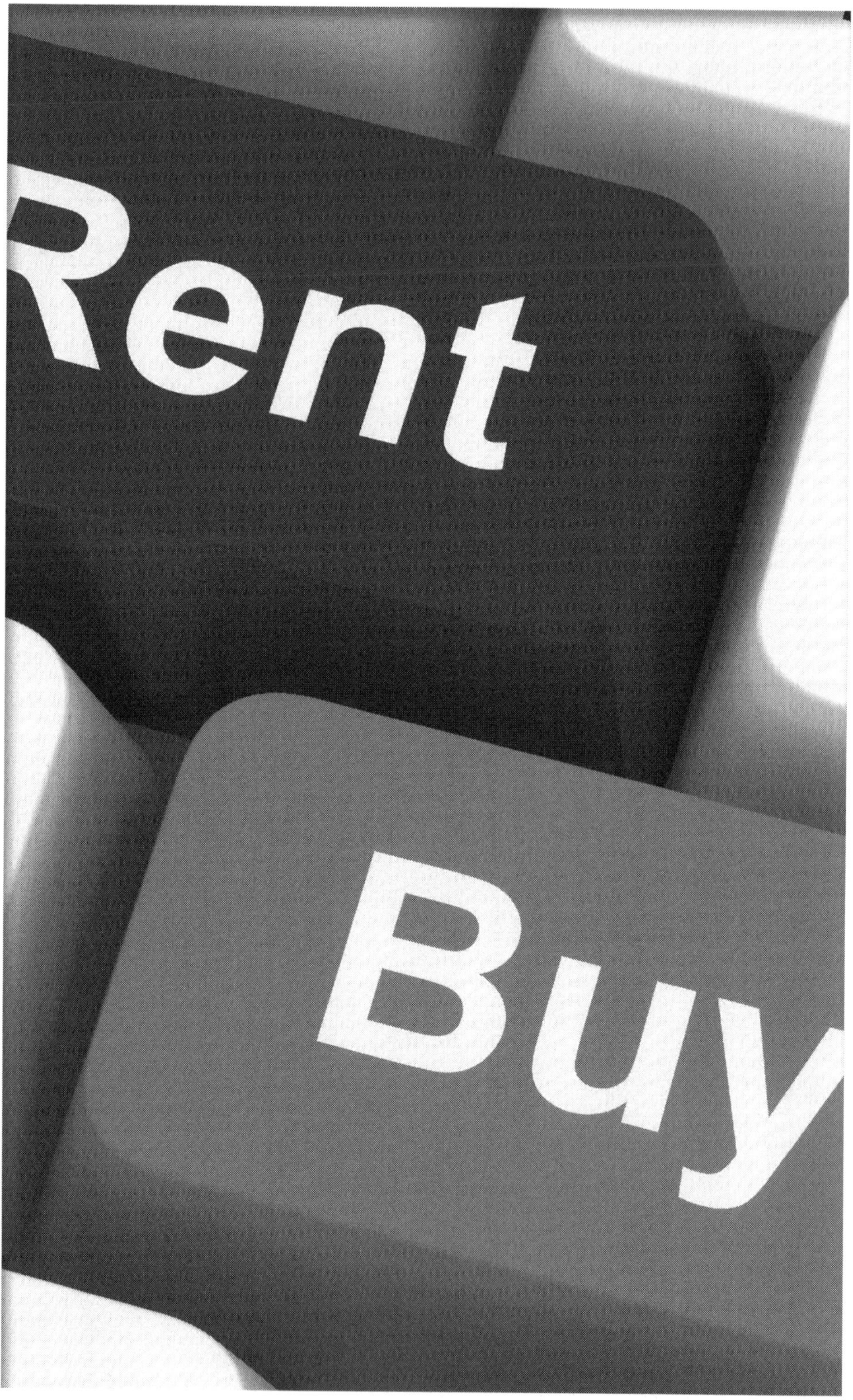
Rent
Buy

CHAPTER 6

Lease Purchases/Owner Financing

The Truth About "No Money Down"

What's so great about this process?

A n entire chapter has been devoted to these two processes because, when applied properly, it can truly a "no or low money down" process. These are also very viable options for first time homebuyers. Both processes require more of your time, but it is a very smart investment market to tap into, especially when the market is slow. On the other hand when the market is on an upswing, and real estate is selling extremely fast it is more challenging to enter into creative financing options, such as these. When sellers can sell a property outright, in their minds it is always better. However, we know that markets go up and down, so I left this chapter in just in case you are in a slow market and will know how to look for these type of investment opportunities.

Here's the difference between the two: a lease-purchase has a lease with an option to purchase, the time-frame is specified upfront. With owner financing, you may only make a down payment and make monthly payments directly to the owner for the duration of the loan. The lender is the owner. Think of this way, the owner has to own the property free and clear to be able to provide this type of financing.

They are very similar in that they both require a contract and specified terms and owner's consideration for it to work.

I purchased a few of investment properties using owner financing. The owner was nearing the end of his career and wanted to move some of his properties. I was able to negotiate a package deal with a balloon payment that worked for both us.

When interest rates are low and people can't sell for what they owe or what they think is fair, to enter into a lease-purchase scenario could work. This could help the existing owner to cover the mortgage debt and qualify for another home; while allowing a first-time homebuyer to enter into a home while working on being able to qualify for a mortgage. It is imperative for you to understand the motivation of what's driving the owner to move; you don't want to find out that they are behind on their mortgage, or that they haven't paid property taxes, or worst and the property is in pre-foreclosure! If you are going to do business with them, you can certainly ask for this type of information.

This method, like all the others, requires persistence: it doesn't just happen. As you find these opportunities, start by finding out some basic information to see this is an ideal property for a lease-purchase. Some recommendations should include:

1) Always start out by ascertaining whether or not it is a good time for the person to talk. Introduce yourself as a real estate investor.

2) Try to find out information about the property first, then discover what is motivating the owner to sell.

3) Ask the owner over the telephone whether or not the property requires work. Most will have some idea of how much the work will cost.

4) Put the idea of a lease-purchase in the owner's head and set up an appointment to speak further about what you do and how you could assist with the sell of the property.

Aspects of the lease-purchase contract:

- ❑ Negotiate sales price
- ❑ Negotiate option money
- ❑ Negotiate monthly payments
- ❑ Negotiate terms
- ❑ Negotiate repairs

A lease-purchase example:

You locate a property online for sale by owner. They are asking $100,000; current market price is $110,000 (reduced for quick sale). The mortgage balance is $80,000, with $700.00 in monthly payments, and the property requires no repairs. Consider that two offers have been made on the property: the first offer was made by you and consists of purchasing the property by way of lease-purchase option. You offer $5,000 down (with this amount being credited to you towards your down payment at closing), with monthly payments of $900.00 and a two-year term, at which time you will buy the property for the asking price of $100,000. The second offer is $90,000, requesting $2,000 to be paid in closing costs, with a 30-day closing period.

> **Real Estate Wealth Tip #23**
>
> *To become wealthy you must understand how to buy property with as little down as possible.*

Your job is to determine whether there are any benefits for the owner in using a lease-purchase contract, and point those benefits out. Through conversation you find out that they have a second home to which they are moving, outside of the city, and they don't want to have to pay mortgages on two properties. With this information, you can now see that they are very good candidates for a lease-purchase, and you should be able to show them how they can make money, instead of selling the property below market value to get a quick sale. The sell offer basically allows them to net $8,000 after closing costs.

The simplified version goes like this: you locate a property that an owner is motivated to sell. Keep in mind that sellers can be anxious to move for several reasons; however, some may just want debt relief. Once again it is your job to find out what they are looking for out of the sale, and from there you can determine if it is something that would benefit all parties. You always want to create a win-win relationship for all parties involved.

Begin by researching the market to determine *what properties in the area would rent for, as well as what properties in the area would sell for.* You should also get an idea of the appreciation rate in the area. Some areas appreciate faster than others do; however, the national average is 4%. Based on your findings, put together at least two different proposals to present to the seller. One, of course, would present your ideal situation, and the other would be an option that you could live with.

The structure of your lease-purchase would look something like this:

Seller/Owner YOU Tenant/ Buyer

❑ The seller wants $5,000 to grant YOU the option to purchase the property in two years.

❑ The tenant-buyer can pay $7,500 for option to purchase.

❑ The seller wants $100,000 for the property.

❑ The tenant-buyer agrees to buy the property for $118,000 within two years. *(Remember that the property is already valued at $110,000, adding 4% appreciation for two years)*

Seller side of the lease-purchase

The mortgage balance has been decreasing steadily over the term of the lease-purchase agreement. In a two-year time frame, let us say that the mortgage balance is now $73,000. In this case they would have made $200.00 in monthly cash flow ($4,800) over two years, with $5,000 down and $27,000 from the sale ($100,000 less $73,000 mortgage balance), less any agreed-upon fees and closing costs being paid at the time of the sale. This equates to a grand total of $36,800 in two years, at $18,400 per year, as opposed to $8,000 from selling the property for $90,000 two years ago! Not to mention, the rental income increases your monthly cash flow.

Investor side of the lease-purchase

Your profit is the difference between the $5,000 that the owner wants down and the $7,500 that you were able to obtain as option money from the tenant-buyer. The total at the time of signing the lease is $2,500. Your monthly cash flow is the difference between what you are paying the seller—$900.00—and what the tenant-buyer is paying in lease payments; that amount is $100.00 over 24 months, totaling $2,400.

The final part is the sale transaction; you have negotiated upfront the future sales price of $118,000. Once you have paid the seller $100,000, your profit is $18,000, less any fees you agreed to pay toward the sale. Your total profit would be around $22,900 over a two-year period.

Where to Locate Tenant-Buyers

A good place to locate tenant-buyers is through mortgage companies, where you can find people who have been told that they need to wait at least 6-24 months before they are eligible to purchase a house. You can also locate tenant-buyers through newspaper advertisements. It is a good idea to have a 24-hour voice message in place to screen calls and provide information about the process and the properties that are available.

There is always a large market for lease-purchase investors, because a lot of people are looking to own homes; however, due to past financial circumstances, they may have to wait a few months. Most people with families would much rather lease-purchase a home than rent until they are able to purchase.

This market responds to the RENT TO OWN or LEASE-PURCHASE options. They also understand that they may have to pay a little bit more for what they want because of their risk.

With the proper systems in place, you should be able to locate a tenant-buyer within thirty days. Investors who focus on this area generally gain an abundance of tenant-buyers, first through advertising, then they begin to locate the properties that fit the individual needs and financial constraints of the tenant-buyer. (A tenant-buyer is a person who is looking to be a short-tenant, converting into a buyer at the end of a specified period).

Real Estate Wealth Tip #24

To become wealthy in performing lease-purchase transactions, you must understand how to locate tenant buyers.

The most challenging part of this process is getting the owner to agree to what you want, which is to have control of the property to lease and sell it to someone else. If they are motivated or understand how they can make more money, the process will be relatively easy to explain.

I have found that it is better to be upfront about this process and let the owner know how you will benefit from the process. Otherwise, they will not be able to understand why you are so willing to help them, and may become suspicious. You don't have to go into exact numbers, but explain the concept, which is simply that you locate properties for people who are having a little trouble financing a house right now. They have money and are willing to pay the rent and forfeit option money if they default. A big key to this process is being able to assure them that you are the person who will be responsible for assuring that payment is made and the property is maintained. If you will be the tenant-buyer, definitely let the owner know, this could help with their comfort level with the process.

You will need to have a good screening system in place to locate good potential candidates.

(More about screening in Chapter 7, Renting and Selling.)

The second part of the transaction looks like this:

SELLER	YOU	TENANT-BUYER
$5,000	$2,500	PAYS $7,500
$100,000	$18,000	PAYS $118,000

There are other ways that you can structure this transaction, as well: you can have the seller agree to sell the property for $5,000 less, contributing the option money toward the closing cost. Or you can take it from your side, thus making $13,000 on the transaction instead of $18,000. I know you are probably asking, "why would you want to do that?" Just remember that the key to these types of transactions is to create a WIN-WIN relationship.

Let's say that the seller/owner makes monthly payments of $700 for the property to the bank. Based on your research (rental market), you determined that you are able to rent the property in the area for $900.00, but because it is a lease-purchase you decide to lease it for a little bit above market rent. You lease the property to a tenant-buyer for $1,000.00.

Tenant-buyers are getting more sophisticated by the day; maybe they are reading this book! They are willing to pay the $7,500.00 that they have been saving to buy a house, but will often request that some of the money go toward their down-payment at the end of the transaction.

"Rent credit" is another popular concept among this group. If you hear this term, it simply means that the tenant-buyer would like some of their monthly payment to go towards the purchase price or down payment on the home. It is common to apply as little as $50.00; it is also common that if you provide this option, you base the credit on rewarding good behavior.

Example: Tell the tenant-buyer that they will receive a $50.00 per month credit if they pay their rent by the first of every month.

At the time of the purchase, you would total the credit and apply it towards their closing cost or down payment, whichever one is specified in the contract. In this example the credit on a 24-month lease option would be $1,200 ($50.00 over 24 months).

Other factors to consider when structuring lease purchases:

Handling Repairs

Request that the tenant-buyer is responsible for the repairs under $100. This will keep them from contacting you for every little thing.

Most importantly, be sure to have it accounted for in the contract, stating how the repair process will be handled. Remember that all negotiating will be done through you.

Lease-purchase contracts work better with fairly new or recently renovated properties. You don't want repairs to become a major factor in the process; this can make for a big headache.

Negotiating time frame

The longer the term you can negotiate with the owner, the better. You can always pay the property off early, but if something does not go as planned, you have control of the property longer. Also, the time frame that you are able to negotiate with your owner will determine the time frame that you can offer to your tenant-buyer.

Say you agree upon a 24-month lease option with the owner, you will have to agree to either an 18 or a 24-month lease with the tenant-buyer. Preferably 18 months to allow yourself enough time to complete the transaction.

The third part of the transaction looks like this:

SELLER	YOU	TENANT BUYER
Payments $900	$100	Pays $1,000
24month option		18-month lease-purchase

*$110,000 represents today's value for the property, and does not take appreciation into account.

**$118,000 represents the appreciated value, modestly compounded over two years.

Real Estate Wealth Tip #25

To become wealthy you must understand the art of negotiation.

Drawbacks

❑ You never actually build assets.

❑ You are responsible for the property and managing the tenants. You can also hire a management company to oversee this process for you.

Note: This type of transaction should be written with a standard sales contract, dated with the two-year date. You should also have a standard sub-lease or rental agreement in place for protection in the event that you have to evict the tenant-buyer. I would recommend that if you are going to pursue this type of investing, you should have a real estate attorney draft your initial set of contracts; after that you can use it over and over. Or you could partner with an investor who does these types of transactions.

The final aspect to note about lease-purchase transactions is to be sure that you file a copy of the agreement with the owner on the title. This is a precaution to protect all parties involved.

Now imagine this same transaction with a seller who has no mortgage on the property. You could see how that would make the deal that much easier to place. As stated, the best places for locating these types of transactions are through the newspapers, by owner, and real estate agents. Real estate agents have listings of people who really need to move for whatever reason: job relocation, new home, or possible foreclosure. If you were planning to work this avenue, it would be a great idea to establish a relationship with a few different agents.

NOTES

CHAPTER 7

Managing And Selling Your Own Properties

Everything You Need To Know

What you should know about managing and selling your own properties.

I n this chapter it will become clear to you that my personal preference is to let the professionals handle their respective areas of expertise. However, if you have the time and expertise then it could work very well for you.

I completely understand how it feels to be a new investor and the desire to learn all the roles associated with the investing process. As you learn more and become experienced, you will be able to determine what works best for you. Let's say that you are a handyman and your spouse is good at bookkeeping, well managing your own properties could certainly work. Whether you decide to manage or sell your own properties will greatly depend on your investment model. You will know what works for you when you see it!

At this point in your investment career, you should set up a Limited Liability Company (LLC) in which to hold your properties. This type of structure has been recommended hands-down by certified public accountants as being the best legal structure for holding real estate.

In many states you can set up any legal entity fairly easily, or you can consult with an accountant.

The main purpose of creating a legal entity is to separate you as an individual from your real estate holdings. This company takes on its own identity and carries its own tax identification number.

Real Estate Wealth Tip#26

Becoming wealthy means understanding that your real estate holdings should be a separate entity from you.

Recommendations:

☐ Obtain a post office box

This will assist you in staying organized. It also keeps you from having to list your home address on any public documents. Remember that you should treat your investment property like the business that it is.

☐ Open a separate bank account

This will allow you to track expenses and make your annual tax preparation much easier. Have any checks related to your properties payable to your LLC, and write checks from this account to cover property expenses. All of the activity from this LLC will transfer to your tax return, and the income, as well as the deductions, will reflect on your personal tax return as business income. In most cases the deductions can be substantial and cause your taxable income to be lowered drastically.

You are also able to build a history in the name of the Limited Liability Company, for when you began purchasing property directly through this entity. This typically takes about 18-24 months, the bank may also require you to be the personal guarantor.

❏ Purchase an accounting software system

This will allow you to track and maintain the expenses associated with your property on a monthly basis. You should definitely try to input the information at least quarterly, if not monthly, so that you don't fall behind.

For your first few properties, it is not necessary to use an accountant if you have a good tracking system. However, after two or more properties, you will probably want to consult with an accountant to ensure that you are maximizing the benefits of investment property ownership.

Another tip is to schedule an appointment with a CPA and let them know that you would like them to assist you in setting up a tracking system. Most CPAs use Quickbooks Professional Series software that you can purchase from any office supply store. Usually they will only charge you a onetime set-up fee and a fee to complete your tax return at the end of the year. Because accounting laws relating to property and taxes are updated so frequently, you want to make sure that you are taking advantage of all of your tax benefits. The most commonly missed deductions by part-time investors are "passive income" and depreciation calculations.

❏ Common Deductions

Listed below are the common deductions associated with owning investment property. However, you should consult with your CPA.

✓ Origination Fees and Points

✓ Interest

✓ Depreciation

✓ Property taxes

✓ Maintenance and repairs

✓ Marketing and advertising

✓ Mileage or gas receipts

✓ Meetings, seminars and products purchased to enhance education in the field

✓ Supplies used in tracking properties (can also include computer, software)

✓ Accounting fees and other consulting fees

❑ Grouping your properties

I recommend that you place no more than five properties in one LLC. Some investors establish a LLC per property. This is all done for liability protection purposes.

This doesn't need to be a complicated process. Keep the same basic name for your LLC and just name them sequentially: Jones LLC, Jones LLC1, Jones LLC2, and so on.

❑ Holding property in a Real Estate Trust

As you began to build your portfolio, you may want to consider holding property in a trust. This process is a little more involved and recommended when there is not a great deal transition involved with your properties (such as selling or re-financing: it is very difficult to re-finance a property that is being held in a trust).

Managing Your Own Properties

Implement a Good Lease

There is no need to re-invent the wheel! Find a good lease that is "state protected," which means that it has all the elements you need if you ever have to go to court to evict a tenant. Tailor the lease to fit your standards and criteria (deposit amount, application fee, what is refundable, and what is not refundable). I was surprised to find out just how smart tenants are, and you certainly don't want them to know more about the leasing process than you do. It is highly recommended that you use a state-endorsed landlord's manual and become familiar with every aspect of your rights as a landlord. I was in a state of disbelief the first time that I had to evict a tenant. I found it a mind-boggling experience to think that someone had been living in my property for a couple of months without paying rent, and I was the one who had to be inconvenienced by going through a horrific court process! (There is a Sample Lease in the *Appendix*.)

Eviction

There are many small steps that must be taken prior to actually evicting a tenant. If you do not follow each step, you can risk having to wait longer to have the tenant evicted. If you find yourself in this situation, follow your state's landlord manual step-by-step. If something seems unusual, consult with a real estate attorney. However, once you get to court the process is pretty cut and dry: either they have paid or they haven't.

It is also important that you have good record-keeping system in place, documenting any conversations regarding payments, maintenance and steps related to the eviction process. When you go to court, be prepared and have all of your facts together.

Note: Know the signs when a tenant begins to fall behind or to pay later than usual. A lot of times, I have found that if you have conversation with them early and agree to let them out of their lease being responsible for only that one month or at most the next month's rent, gets them off the hook and allow you to look for another tenant. This is better than waiting until they owe you for two months, then going to court, losing another 30-days, not to mention the frustration.

Implement a good screening system

This is an important phase that a lot of investors miss, once again because they are anxious. Most feel that they don't have the time or the money to implement this system. There are several companies, which perform screening services for a minimal fee. These services provide you with a background check, credit check and a criminal report. You can request all of the reports or just the ones that you are most interested in. Although I might not base my decision on all of the reports, I would request them for my files (I would definitely want to know if there was a criminal staying on my property). This fee can be transferred to the prospective tenant in the form of an application fee, so you really aren't paying for it anyway. Standard application fees are anywhere from $25.00-$125.00. Yes, there can be a reasonable mark-up for your time; believe it or not, you can obtain a credit report from all three bureaus for as little as $14.00. You can also do simple things for your protection, such as having the prospective tenant obtain his or her criminal record from the police station. Make sure that the county or state seals it; this report should include all criminal activity statewide. If someone has just recently moved into the state, you may also want to request a criminal background for the previous state as well. Finally, call references and work information mainly for verification and limited character information.

Implement a move-in/move-out checklist system

This helps you to control your property and ascertain whether something is damaged or missing at the time the tenant moves out. The checklist should be signed by both parties and list any concerns at the time of moving in. It is important that you don't get into a big hurry during the tenant move-in phase. This happens often, and results in investors failing to have this document in place. If you allow the tenant to move in before you complete a thorough walkthrough of the property, it will be your word against theirs if something is damaged before they have moved in completely. Keep this document in the tenant's file. You should complete a move-out checklist as well. You will then be able to compare the two, as well as the condition of the property. These forms are good for justifying why you are retaining some of their deposit, and how much. I also recommend taking interior photos prior to the tenant moving in, for your files. There is a sample checklist in the *Appendix*.

Implement a good tracking system

It is important that you have a good tracking system in place. Keeping up with a mortgage payment, an insurance and tax payment requires a systematic process. It is equally important to have these expenses for tax purposes. Keep records of all of your receipts, invoices and any other costs associated with the property. At the end of the year you will be able to go to your documentation to prepare your taxes yourself, or to deliver the file to your C.P.A. There is a sample tracking form in the *Appendix*.

Set up a 24-hour telephone number or email address for non-emergency situations

Having tenants means that there is no predictable time for problems. Tenants like to be able to reach you or at least leave a message, 24 hours a day. Be sure to establish a system for handling maintenance calls, and address turn-around times and expectations up front. This way, everyone will know what to expect, and it will cut down on the amount of interaction you will need to have with the tenants. For example, it may be your policy that all minor repair calls are handled within 72 hours of the report date. Be sure to define minor repairs and give the tenant notice of how you will handle repairs, either in the lease or as a separate handout at the time of move-in. On the other hand, emergency repairs should be handled within 24 hours of the report date. Emergencies may include not having heat or AC, it would also include not having a working toilet if there is only one in the home.

Note: Make sure that you request renters insurance from your tenant, it's for their protection but things can get very gray when things go wrong with the property.

Implement a system for showing your property

Whether you are renting or selling buyers will need to get inside to view the property. Here are a few suggestions:

Ask a neighbor who is at home during the day to look after the property for you and go over and show the property for you. Offer to give him or her a small fee for his or her time.

Depending on the area, you can place a coded lockbox on the door with the key inside it. When prospects who fit the criteria call, you can give them the code and ask them to replace the key when they leave the property. When doing this, it is good practice to go by the property fairly regularly and change the code.

Although time does not always permit, it is good practice to meet prospects in person. You are able to get a better feel about the person during a face-to-face meeting. Be sure to take someone with you.

Real Estate Wealth Tip #27

To become wealthy you must put a good system in place to screen and locate tenants, show property and collect payments effectively.

Tips:

✓ When managing your own properties, I would recommend not telling the tenants that you are the owner. Experience has taught me that this is better. My favorite line was always "I have to check with the owner."

✓ Don't get to know your tenants on a personal basis. They will feel too close to you, and every time something goes wrong with their finances, they think you'll understand.

✓ Begin looking for a tenant towards the end of your rehab phase. Also start advertising the property as soon as it looks presentable and is safe to enter.

✓ You should keep a separate bank account to hold tenant deposits. Also, find out whether your state requires you to hold this money in an interest-bearing account. This way, when your tenants move out, your accounting system is in place.

Selling Your Own Properties

When you are selling your own properties, remember that you are writing a contract that should be to your advantage. To ensure that you don't miss any steps, I recommend using a standard state purchase sale contract. You can cross out anything that you don't want included and use the stipulation section for any additions. There is a sample contract in the *Appendix* for you to view. However, make sure that you find one that is specific to your state. They are relatively easy to find online.

The basic parts of the contract include:

- ☐ Date contract was entered into
- ☐ Property address and description
- ☐ Contract price
- ☐ Type and terms of the loan
- ☐ Amount and holder of earnest money
- ☐ Date transaction will be closed
- ☐ Signatures of both parties

You should request a letter from the buyer's mortgage company, stating that they are qualified to purchase the property for the amount of the contract. You will also need this information to be able to follow up with their lender with regard to the status of the loan.

Now that you know how to do it yourself, allow me to share with you what to expect from the professionals.

Management Companies and Real Estate Agents

What to look for?

Once again, get referrals from other investors. Good management companies will have processes in place, which enable them to rent the property quickly. You want a management company that will handle all the facets of the management process, are professional and have good systems in place. Over the last several years, we have seen a more popular trend for agents specializing in rental property. Most of them have very good systems for locating tenants fast and will charge one full month of the rent to manage the property for the year. This is usually done for properties that don't require a lot of maintenance. However, look into this process as well, and figure out what works best for you.

How much should you expect to pay?

Most management companies will charge an acquisition fee for locating a tenant. This fee mainly comprises reimbursement for advertising and expenses, which arise from acquiring the tenant. A monthly management fee is also charged, based on the amount of rent that is collected. This can be anywhere from 5-15%, depending on the company.

The relationship with your management company should be well defined beforehand: its role, the time frame and the cost should be negotiated upfront in a written contract. Most management companies will only contract for 90-120 days to have your property rented. You do not want to enter into a contract for any longer than that.

At minimum you should expect the management company to locate a tenant in a timely manner, perform walkthroughs and show the property to prospective tenants. Once a tenant has been secured, they should execute the lease and process all payments and take maintenance calls. The management company should also handle evictions and rent demands on your behalf.

Tip:

Whether you are managing your properties yourself or using a management company, it is imperative that you have a reserve of at least $2,500 per property, or three months' worth of payments, whichever is higher. This is your rainy-day fund, to be used for minor maintenance, vacancy payments, and emergencies. Always replenish this fund to maintain whatever is used. This will save you a lot of grief.

NOTES

the following

Amex (A) ☐ Diners (D) ☐ Connect ☐

Financial Details

MONTHLY INCOME

Your earnings after tax

CHAPTER 8

Financing Options

Where And How To Obtain Financing

Find out what you want and where to go to get it.

T he biggest myth about banks is that investors need them! In actuality, banks need investors to borrow money, pay interest and to get into debt, which is essentially what you will be doing. Even though you will certainly be doing all of these things, you are learning to do them in a controlled and calculated way.

Putting Debt Into Perspective

As an investor it is imperative that you grasp the concept of debt. Not all debt is bad debt. In a sense, debt can be a negative or a positive, depending on which side you are on. Consider your primary home, even though it takes money out of your pocket, the end result is that it is something that you need. A need that you can afford, the alternative is that you could pay hundreds of thousands of dollars renting over a long period of time without anything to show for it.

On the other hand, your rental property is considered "good debt": you can earn extra money from it. Or at least use the rental payment to pay your mortgage, taxes and insurance, every month. Rental property allows someone else to pay the property off for you. By putting debt in its proper perspective, you will not be afraid of getting into a little of it. As matter of fact, you should start to feel as if you can't get into debt fast enough!

There are several ways of obtaining financing for purchasing investment properties. This chapter will assist you in finding the best channel(s) for you. This chapter will also explore information and tips on obtaining financing from banks, credit unions, mortgage companies, hard-money lenders as well as owner-financing. Each investor has a different set of needs, and finding the best financing structure for you is to your advantage.

Banks

What to expect?

When you go to the bank to inquire about getting a loan for an investment property, be very specific about what you want. Banks, for the most part, are rigid, and the programs they offer are limited. I suggest going to the website or speaking with a loan officer by telephone to gain information about the various programs available prior to visiting. Doing a little homework upfront will enable you to go in armed with knowledge about their loan requirements and programs. You can also put together a plan that combines what the bank has to offer with what you are looking to obtain. This will make your visit very productive.

Next, you will want to show how both you and the bank can make money through your efforts. Remember that the bank is going to be one of your "team members" during your investment career, so everyone must make money in order for the relationship to work. It is important to build a good foundation by developing a rapport and by letting the bank officer know your full investment plans. Bank officers *should understand how many properties you want to purchase, the time frame in which you would like to acquire them, an estimate of your cost per property, and also the expected profit.* Demonstrate that you have a plan and that you are ambitious, but don't overwhelm them. You don't want them to feel that your over-zealousness can be costly to them.

You should be able to exemplify that you are clear and educated about what you are looking to do, or it will be virtually impossible to convince the bank to loan you hundreds of thousands of dollars!

I have seen investors go into banks completely unprepared. Bankers are very limited when it comes to their time and lack imagination, so get to the point and make your plan plain and understandable. They are simply not going to spend a lot of time trying to figure out what you want to do.

Lately, there have been more and more small banks entering the market. These banks operate aggressively with small town flair, and are usually very practical and fast in-house. Small banks are looking for opportunity, and are more willing to take a chance on a person or project. Once you have built a good rapport, they tend to move extremely fast and are anxious to lend you more money.

Drawbacks

❑ Very specific programs.

Limited room for negotiation on rates, terms, etc.

❑ Credit-driven.

If your credit is less than perfect, banks are not very forgiving of a flawed credit background. You either fit or you don't, without much leeway.

❑ Employee turnover is high

You establish a relationship with one bank officer, only to find out that he or she has been transferred to another branch, or, worse, has left the company.

❑ Highly collateral-driven.

If you have other property or assets that can be used as leverage, you are halfway there in the banking industry.

More on banks

On the other hand, banks are excellent sources of equity lines when you are starting out. It is a good idea to go to your bank and apply for an equity line of credit from your primary home, if equity is available. A lot of new investors get money from their primary home to use for making down payments and covering renovation costs. I highly recommend this as an option for cash flow and reserves to get started.

Credit Unions

What to expect?

Credit unions are usually stricter than banks with regard to their lending practices and real estate investing guidelines. However, once again, credit unions are an excellent source for equity lines. If you have established a relationship, it is not as difficult to obtain a loan.

To be a member of a credit union, you must have some affiliation with a member company. For example, you may work for a company that is a member of a credit union. This type of relationship is based on commonality—you have something in common, so you are given access to the perks that come with being a member of a credit union. If you belong to a credit union, it probably won't be a main source of money to purchase investment property. They prefer to stick with primary financing. However, they are an excellent source for consulting about a second mortgage, line of credit or financing a vehicle!

It is important that you research all of your options and examine the relationships that you have had over the last few years with various financial institutions. Once you understand where each entity fits into what you are trying to do, you will have a better picture of how you can use each one.

Mortgage Companies

What to expect?

This is your most flexible source of financing. The best part is that once you locate a mortgage broker, he or she has access to hundreds of lenders who have different programs and guidelines available to investors.

Your mortgage broker can find you the best rate and term to fit your individual needs. Once again it is important that he or she understands your investment plans in order to provide you with advice and strategies.

It is equally important that your broker knows what you are planning to do with each piece of property that you purchase. The broker should be able to determine the best-fit loan for the property. As opposed to a banker, a broker usually has more time to sit down and understand your long-term goals. Let's assume that you are purchasing a property to renovate and sell. You would not want to have a pre-payment penalty attached to the loan (a pre-payment penalty is when you are penalized for paying your loan off early). Make sure that your broker is exploring all of the options available to you, so that you can make the best decision. I have known investors who did not want to share with their mortgage broker their exact plans for the property. In the end they became upset with the broker for not pointing out certain drawbacks or disadvantages to a particular loan program. Don't make this mistake!

Understanding mortgage companies

Mortgage companies react to the ever-changing industry. Look for a mortgage broker who stays involved within the industry. This means that he or she is always aware of new programs and legislation that may affect you as an investor. Programs change very frequently when losses in certain areas are higher than normal or when lenders are exposed to risk, for example. There are a number of reasons for this rapidly changing industry.

Understanding interest rates

Interest rates are determined through the Federal Reserve. The federal lending rate drives the secondary market interest rates. Money is sold at 0.5 to 20 times higher than the amount it is purchased for on the open market. Interest rates from mortgage companies are normally higher than the rates you can obtain from a bank or credit union. Typically, investors' interest rates are anywhere from 1-4% higher than the prime rate. Investment property rates are higher because of the associated risk. You may not consider yourself to be a risk, but lenders do because they know that anything can happen in the market. These rates are higher as well, because this is considered a secondary market. Mortgages are sold in bundles to the open stock market through investment companies. In order to make a profit, lenders charge mortgage companies above the prime rate. Lenders sell their loans to replenish their capital to continue making loans to mortgage companies.

Lenders are the source from which mortgage brokers obtain their money. Certain lenders are willing to assume higher credit risk; however, they will charge you for it in the interest rate. When your circumstances start to improve, the interest rates offered to you will begin to reflect the improvement.

A typical loan structure is based on what is called loan-to-value (LTV). This is the information that you will receive, based on credit and other factors used by the various lenders. The amount of money the bank will loan you will help you determine how much of your own money you will need to put into purchasing the property.

With all of this being said, so much has changed with lending practices since the real estate crash that took place in 2007-2009. Loan-to-values are now pretty consistent for investors; anywhere from 70-80%. Most lenders will expect for you to be able to make a down payment of at least 20% into the transaction. For example, if the property is $100,000 and the mortgage company is financing the property at 80%, you will be responsible for $20,000. This is also where owner financing could come in. The lender is basically saying that all that we will contribute to the deal is 80% however, you could structure a loan where you pay 10% down and the owner holds a note for the other 10%. Always negotiate your contract so that the seller is paying a large part of the closing cost, especially if there is no owner financing involved. This will keep your out-of-pocket costs down. You may be buying a property that requires repairs, but once they are complete, in most cases the value of the property should increase by at least 20%. You can then refinance to obtain some, if not all, of your down-payment money back.

For example, the property is now valued at $135,000, after the repairs have been completed. At 80% refinance, $108,000 after paying off the original loan of $80,000 and closing costs estimated at 3% or $3,240, you will be left with $24,760. In this example, the down payment was $20,000 and let's says that the repairs were $4,000. The total out-of-pocket cost is $24,000. The most important part to this refinance is that you replenish as much of your investment money as possible. If this refinance transaction is done within a short time frame, you will probably have to produce receipts or canceled checks showing the amount of work and improvements that have been made to the property. Your broker should be able to explain this type of situation further. Again, it is imperative that you let them know that this is what you are trying to accomplish so that you will get all of the information upfront and there are no surprises.

Rates and risk

As stated earlier, interest rates on investment properties are slightly higher.

My opinion on interest rates is that they should be relative to what you are making on the transaction. Besides, you can always re-finance to obtain a lower rate.

Remember that you are ultimately the person who is taking all of the risk, so be sure to obtain a clear understanding of the programs and your options. A lack of understanding can lead to a potentially bad situation. You cannot trust that the mortgage broker is always going to have your best interests at heart, so know what questions to ask and do your own homework. Make sure that you review all of the paperwork regarding your loan terms prior to closing.

> ### Real Estate Wealth Tip #29
>
> *To become wealthy you must understand the different types of lending institutions and loans that are available to you.*

Drawbacks

There are not many drawbacks to using mortgage companies, because they are able to accommodate almost anybody. Even negative credit situations are more workable in this arena than any other financial institutions.

Mortgage companies are a lot more forgiving when it comes to late payments, bankruptcy, and so on.

One minor drawback is that mortgage companies typically only finance property that is habitable. There are a few conventional programs available that are targeted toward renovating properties, due to the revitalization surge. However, most of these programs are designed for primary residents and are not available for investment properties.

Interest rates may be a little higher.

When you are purchasing property that will require more than minor or cosmetic repairs, you will need to consider financing from a hard-money lender. Frankly, I have never known why they are referred to as hard-money lenders, because it is not hard to obtain money from them it's just expensive!

Hard-Money Lenders

What to expect?

Hard-money lenders deal primarily with investment property (residential and commercial).

These lenders can structure loans very fast; the turnaround time is incredible. Since they are private, they are not regulated by normal banking guidelines. Their procedures, interest rates and forms can be of their own design. This type of lender is taking on a different kind of risk than your average lending institution. This means, in turn, that interest rates are higher than average. The types of loans that these lenders provide are based on the after-repair value (ARV) of the property. Typically, a loan from a hard-money lender includes the amount of the property, along with the amount of the repairs. Hard-money lenders trust that you will complete the repairs in a timely manner. These lenders view every piece of property that they provide financing for. They have their own certified appraisers who establish the ARV for the property. These certified appraisers work for the lender, and it is their job to protect them. Therefore, they are very conservative with values in working to minimize the bank's risk. The appraiser calculates the value based on the amount of the repairs to be performed. Before this appraisal can be done, you will have to provide a list of improvements that will be done to increase the value. Be sure that you can trust whoever is giving you this estimate, if you did not obtain it yourself. Remember that you are the only responsible party, so if you go to the bank and do not ask for enough money, this may pose a major problem for you!

Hard-money lenders are more concerned with the value of the property once the repairs have been completed. In the event that the investor defaults on the loan, they want to know that it is still profitable.

When deciding whether to use a hard-money lender, first you must find out about their lending structure. These lenders will loan 65%-70% of the ARV. Based on this loan structure, you will take the purchase price and the amount of estimated repairs to figure out whether you will be able to use hard money.

For example, the property that you are looking to purchase costs $75,000. The cost of the repairs is estimated at $25,000 (including your contingency factor). Next, determine the estimated ARV, and subtract 10% from your number (the appraisal will always be conservative). If you determine this number to be $150,000, 65% is $97,500. At this point you need $100,000 to make the purchase ($75,000 plus $25,000). With the amount of the loan at $97,500, you are short by $2,500. You have to be willing to put up the difference of $2,500, plus the closing costs (which are also higher when using hard money), and don't forget that you will have to make monthly payments. You have to account for all your costs when analyzing any real estate transaction, but when using hard money with a 10-18% interest rate, you need to be on the mark with the numbers.

Another example: your total closing cost (including the $2,500 difference) is $7,300; monthly payments are $1,000. You have planned for renovations and market time of 180 days, and therefore have a reserve for payments of a minimum of $6,000. In this example, your total out-of-pocket expenses will be approximately $13,300, and the loan is for $97,500. The total investment in the property is $110,800.

We determined earlier that $150,000 is the ARV for the property, less $110,800 total investment required; your potential profit would then be $39,200. In this case, if you use hard-money, it would be fine; that is, as long as you have the $13,300 out-of-pocket investment.

Some transactions can be structured so that the out-of-pocket is very limited. This would mean that the ARV is high enough to incorporate the majority of your cost into the loan. Because this money is so expensive, I highly recommend that you always work based on the worst-case scenario. For example, what if it takes nine months to renovate and sell the property instead of the anticipated six months? In this case your holding cost will be a lot higher: $9,000 instead of $6,000, thus taking an additional $3,000 from your profit line. If you only have $13,300 and don't have a clue where you will get additional money if necessary, I would recommend that you think twice about undertaking this type of transaction, or perhaps think about "partnering".

Other considerations:

If the property stays on the market longer than expected, you can always lower the price. You will still have some room and be able to make a decent profit. For example, you might lower the price from $150,000 to $140,000, still yielding a profit of $29,200.

Say, after all of your planning and figuring, your rehab cost is still over by $3,000, this will have to come from you to complete the job, meaning that your profit line will decrease by this amount.

I am spending a lot of time on hard-money transactions, because they have been known to get a lot of investors into trouble and have contributed to the downfall of many.

There are many aspects to consider when using hard-money, because these lenders are very unforgiving when you fail to make a monthly payment. Most hard-money foreclosures take place within 45 days of the first payment being missed. This is why they are so conservative in estimating the ARV, in case they have to foreclose on the property. They want to make sure that they have plenty of equity for a quick sale if necessary.

More on hard money lenders

Repairs are handled through a draw system. Once work has been completed and inspected by the lender, a check will be cut based on the work that was done. This means that you will have to have some money to get the job started for material etc...most subcontractors understand that they won't be paid until work is completed.

Other reasons why people use hard-money:

❑ Most hard-money lenders do not record mortgages on your credit. These are private lenders and are not required by law to do so.

❑ It's a good idea to use hard-money lenders when re-selling property for short-term transactions.

❑ Hard-money is good to use when you are purchasing a property that requires a lot of work.

❑ You can also use a combination of loans: borrow through hard-money to complete repairs and then refinance as a conventional loan when finished.

❑ Most of the time, these loans do not have associated prepayment penalties because they are short-term. However, be mindful that they do exist.

❑ As with any other form of lending institution, you can establish a good working relationship.

Seasoning is another mortgage term that you will hear which tells the lender how long the property has been owned by you; for example, the property has three months' seasoning. Sometimes, it is good to use hard-money lenders, or pay cash for property because this doesn't come up as a barrier.

Additional Financing Information

Points and Fees

With any loan you should expect to pay points and fees. Your banker, loan officer or hard-money lender is just like any other professional, paid for his or her time and knowledge in the respective field. You will need to have a clear understanding of the points and fees being charged.

A point is defined as 1% of the loan amount. For example, on a loan amount of $100,000, one point would be $1,000; two points would be $2,000. Points are also represented as origination fees. These terms are used interchangeably in the mortgage and banking industry.

Banks and Credit Unions

The points associated with the loan process are minimal. These institutions usually charge lower loan origination fees, as the processing involved with their loans is pretty basic. Most of the loan process is done in-house, and bankers are paid an incentive in addition to their salary to complete loans. Fees associated with these institutions are also minimal. These fees are usually flat and are a cost of doing any loan, not dependent on loan size. There are several other fees associated with any loan, such as insurance, appraisal, title, and, of course, taxes.

Overall these institutional points and fees are low, and most are not negotiable.

Mortgage Companies

Points associated with mortgage companies are generally a little higher, mainly because there is a tier system involved. With loans that are considered to be "brokered," the loan officer is paid, as well as the broker. Most importantly, mortgage companies operate on commission only. If a loan does not close, this means that no one is paid. Loan officers work twice as hard as bank or credit union officers do. They are looking for the best fit for your loan, which means that they are using a process known as "shopping" your loan. Shopping is locating the best interest rate on the market, as well as trying to obtain the highest loan-to-value available.

Points at a mortgage company are usually between 1-3% of the loan amount. Remember, with this process broker fees as well as lender fees are charged in addition to the standard fees associated with any loan.

Also remember that sometimes you pay a little more for knowledge and expertise. Cheaper is not always better. Just make sure that you understand each fee that is on your "Good Faith Estimate" and your "Truth-In-Lending". These are the two most important documents outlining the numbers associated with the loan.

Good Faith Estimate (GFE)

There is a sample GFE in the *Appendix*. This form is a required loan document that should be prepared within three days of making a loan request. The GFE provides you with a breakdown of your points and fees, and also shows the estimated taxes, insurances, attorney fees, title fees and appraisal fees. In addition, it will provide you with the amount of money you should expect to have as a down payment. The GFE should mirror the Settlement Statement when you go to the final closing. If the GFE changes by $100.00, up or down, you should be provided with an updated copy.

In my opinion, this is the most important document to have when entering into a relationship with a financier. It is also the most important document to use in order to gain a comprehensive understanding of the numbers associated with your loan.

Truth-In-Lending (TIL)

This document discloses information about the interest rate, whether the loan is fixed or adjustable, the total amount that will be paid in interest, and the total cost over the life of the loan. It is also essential that you understand this document.

Settlement Statement (HUD 1)

The closing attorney provides this statement as part of the closing package. Usually it is available 24 hours prior to closing. However, if your mortgage broker or banker did a good job of keeping you informed throughout the process, there should be no surprises here. The Good Faith Estimate and the Settlement Statement should be pretty close to exact. The only difference is that the GFE is an estimate and the Settlement Statement reflects the actual charges associated with the loan.

See the *Appendix* for a sample of a Good Faith Estimate, as well as a Truth In Lending Disclosure Statement. As an investor, these documents should not be foreign to you. They should become part of your learning process; this will enable you to pick out red flags regarding your loan.

Fixed vs. Adjustable Rate Mortgages (ARM)

There are two important aspects to any loan:

❑ What is the interest rate for the loan?

❑ What are the terms of the loan?

The interest rate in a fixed mortgage remains constant for the life of the loan. The most common terms for a fixed mortgage are 180 months (15-year) or 360 months (30-year).

Adjustable rate mortgages (ARMs) can have a variety of different interest rates and terms. Because these loans are only guaranteed for a specified period, the interest rate is lower. The loan could have a fixed interest rate for 1 year, 3 years, or 5 years. This simply means that during this particular period of time, the rate can't change; however, after this time period, the rate can adjust, based on the type of loan, every month or every year thereafter.

Based on your plans for the property, you may want to consider using an ARM for houses that you will re-sell within a short period of time. As stated, ARMs usually have a lower interest rate initially, which is adjusted higher at the end of the stated time frame. It is also good to make use of ARMs if your credit is not so good when you are first starting out. This type of loan will allow you to get into a mortgage at a lower interest. Once your credit situation starts to improve and your payment history is good, you can re-finance the property into a fixed loan or review other options.

When interest rates are low, it is always good to consider fixed rates, this way no matter what you decide to do with the property, you are covered. When rates are low, it is also a good time to consider 180 month (15 year) mortgages. In most cases you can pay off a house in less than 10 years with this type of mortgage in place. Imagine if you currently have an 8% interest rate and you are able to go to a 5% interest rate, your payments will be close to the same. If you pay an additional $100 a month towards the principal, you will be amazed at how quickly you can pay off the loan. This arrangement is best to consider when entering into a long-term contract.

Tip:

You can accelerate a 30-year mortgage by paying over the requested amount each month. You can accelerate the loan by simply sending one additional payment each year. This additional payment is all applied to the principal of the loan, thus cutting your loan term. *(Note: you must designate how you would like the extra payment to be applied).*

Interest-only loans

Interest-only loans are quickly becoming increasingly a thing of the past. This type of loan will significantly lower your monthly payments, thereby increasing your monthly cash flow. This loan works very well in many cases. I encourage you to gain a good understanding of this type of loan by consulting with your mortgage broker, as well as inquiring about qualifying requirements.

Qualifying your lending source

Ask the following questions:

- ☐ Do you provide lending for investment properties?
- ☐ What is your experience with working with investor loans?
- ☐ What types of programs do you have available to investors?
- ☐ What is the interest rate on your investment products?
- ☐ What type of credit does your company typically work with?
- ☐ Is there a limit on the number of investment properties that I can finance with your company?
- ☐ How much of my own money will I need to put down?
- ☐ What type of financing terms do you offer?
- ☐ How much will you charge to do the loan?
- ☐ What other fees will be associated with the loan?
- ☐ What will be my up-front cost associated with the loan?
- ☐ Do you recommend any other sources for loans that you do not offer?
- ☐ How do you handle rehab properties?
- ☐ Are you familiar with how to set up subordinate financing or owner financing?
- ☐ Do you offer equity lines of credit?

These questions should get you thinking about your options and which financial institution best suits your investment plans. Remember above all, it is your loan and you are the only person responsible for it. With that being said, do your homework and buy some property!

Real Estate Wealth Tip #30

To become wealthy in real estate you must also become extremely systematic!

Appendices List

Writing Your Real Estate Plan

Writing your Real Estate Plan is the most important part of your investing career. Spend some time working on developing a plan that fits what you want to accomplish. Don't be surprised if it takes some time to really put this together. Remember that it is being designed to guide your investment decisions. Also remember, whatever you decide· **stick to your plan!**

On the next few pages is a sample transaction designed to show you steps and numbers. Plug in your own numbers and follow the same steps each time. You will become a master at the numbers!

Note: The numbers that are represented in this Real Estate Plan will vary greatly if you are purchasing a property to live in. Mainly because your down payment will be so much lower. Either way, this will serve you as a good guide for the process.

Understanding Your Goal

Let's say your goal is to purchase 4 investment properties. Your first 2 will be buy/sell to build up my cash. Then you would like to purchase 2 properties for buy/hold purposes. This will be done over a period of 2 years. Your goal is to accumulate a minimum of $30,000 from sales.

You will get the $25,000 for initial investment from your equity line and re-pay after your first deal.

Or

Your goal is to purchase one investment property as a buy/sell for retirement planning and generational wealth building.

You have $25,000 in cash separate from other reserves to invest.

Your real estate plan would sound something like this:

Consideration #1—Financial Position

Down Payment:

This Plan is based on a beginning investment of at least $25,000. If you have less and there is no way to obtain the $25,000 I would recommend looking for a partner, or looking for a property that you can get into with a lower upfront investment, such as an owner-financing deal or lease-purchase. The beauty of investing in real estate is that there is always more than one way to get started.

Consideration #2—Investment Criteria

#1. Current value of $75,000 or less

#2. ARV of minimum $100,000

#3. Repairs under $10,000

Or

Current value has an equity margin after repairs of at least 25%, requiring $10,000 or less in repairs. Remember, the investment criteria is something that you set.

Consideration #3—Credit Position

Minimum credit score of 720 to be able to qualify for an 80% loan to value structure. Check with your lender some are allowing 680.

Or

A credit score that would allow you to qualify for a 80% loan to value, with 10% owner financing available. Which would mean your total out of pocket would be 10%. If you don't have the qualifying score for this transaction but you have a substantial down payment, you may want to consider finding a partner, who could qualify for the loan or you opt to take a lower loan to value to compensate for not having the required credit criteria.

Consideration #4—Investment Strategy

Buy-Hold strategy with occasional refinances to replenish investment as well to boost cash flow (refer to Chapter 2).

Consideration #5—Available Time

This is probably the hardest part of the plan: being realistic about how much time you really have available to spend investing. This plan is designed for someone who is looking to invest part-time or full-time. Whether purchasing one property or ten, only you can determine what is realistically fits your plan.

Once you understand how you would like real estate to fit into your overall wealth plan, this process becomes much easier. Maybe, after reading this book, you only want to purchase a property with an investor thought process, live in it, sell it after a couple of years to boost your retirement funds. Then purchase another home to live in. Or, maybe, you keep the first home as a rental property to create monthly long-term cash flow as well as create generational wealth by leaving an appreciating asset to your family. With real estate, the sky can be the limit!

Recap of Real Estate Investment Plan:

We have determined that we must be able to qualify for at least an 80% loan. We have $15,000 available for down-payment, plus another $10,000 for repairs and holding costs or we at least know where we will obtain the money for the investment. We also know that we need to have at least 25% equity (ARV) in the property to refinance. This is important to note because our investment strategy is to buy-hold, which is also a characteristic of a long-term investor type (LTI).

Investment Matrix

TIME	10 hours per month (looking for a deal)	Good
MONEY	$25,000	Good
CREDIT	720	Excellent
STRATEGY	Buy/Hold/Refinance	
BUYING PLAN	1 property	

Overview of Transaction

$105,000	ARV
$75,000	Asking price
$70,000	Contract price
$56,000	80% Loan to value
$14,000	Down payment
$8,000	Estimated repairs
$3,000	Available for payments, reserves, holding cost

*Example based on 6.5% interest rate, with 3 months at $750 (and 10% repair reserve)

Steps in Transaction

Step 1: Complete the purchase of the property and the repairs.

Step 2: As we learned in Chapter 7, begin looking aggressively for a tenant when the repair phase is almost completed, or have a management company or system in place to secure a tenant as fast as possible.

Step 3: Upon repairs being completed, begin refinancing the transaction.

The purchase transaction is based on the seller paying all of the closing costs, or you financing them into your loan.

Re-finance Transaction:

$105,000	ARV
$84,000	80% re-finance (usually the maximum amount that you can obtain on an investment property)
*-$2,500	Closing costs estimated at 3% (always figured on the loan amount)
*-$56,000	Loan amount to pay off
$25,000	Initial investment (or whatever amount was actually used)

**$500 Profit*

* Be sure that there are no pre-payment penalties when executing this type of transaction.

* 3% is the estimated closing cost of the total loan, rounded to the nearest one-hundredth. (Could be lower)

* Tax-free because this is a re-finance transaction and not a sale.

Now that you have recouped most if not all of your investment, you can decide on your next move.

We have our initial investment back and the property rented for $950.00 per month. Mortgage payments are calculated to be $750.00 (taxes and insurance). The rental income is $200.00 per month and $2,400 annually.

[Equity position is $21,000 calculated with $105,000 ARV less mortgage balance of $84,000]

Two things to note:

This transaction may take six months to complete, depending on the re-financing (or seasoning) guidelines in your state—*Refer back Chapter 8 Financing.* If this is the case, you will still want to locate a tenant rapidly for the property. By having the property rented by the time you go to re-finance, you are viewed more favorably by the lender because the property is already producing income. In addition, by securing a tenant rapidly, you won't have to make as many payments on the property.

Secondly, by re-financing, you will not realize capital gain taxes on the property.

However, let's consider that your investment strategy is to buy/sell. In this case, we are able to sell the property for $100,000, taking into account some closing costs, etc..., to be contributed by you to the buyer. At $100,000, your profit would look like this:

$100,000	Contract price
-$56,000	Pay off
-$25,000	Initial investment plus holding cost of $3,000
-$7,000	(7% in listing and closing fees)
$12,000	**Profit**

Remember: You can do several things to increase your profit, refer to Chapters 5 and 7 Additional Info based on Rental Scenario:

Amortization Schedule

This following table was done on Bankrate.com at a 4% appreciation rate for property appreciation over 30 years. You could use an even more conservative number like 2% and you will be astounded by how this process works. Keep in mind that the most important things about what this chart displays is the following:

✓ You have an asset that is increasing in value

✓ You have a mortgage loan that is decreasing and more importantly

✓ You have a tenant that is covering this expense on your behalf

✓ You have an asset that when it's time for your child to go to college, you could use some of the equity.

✓ You have an asset that when it's time for you to retire, you can decide whether you want keep this property for enhanced monthly cash flow, or sale the property at say year 15 and cash out about $54,000!

✓ Or, keep the asset and build generational wealth!

Amortization Schedule

	Property Value	Mortgage Balance	Equity Position
Year 1	$105,000.00	$84,000.00	$21,000.00
Year 2	$109,200.00	$83,141.00	$26,059.00
Year 3	$113,568.00	$82,145.00	$31,423.00
Year4	$118,110.72	$81,082.00	$37,028.72
Year 5	$122,835.15	$79,947.00	$42,888.15
Year 6	$127,748.55	$78,737.00	$49,011.55
Year 7	$132,858.50	$77,446.00	$55,412.50
Year 8	$138,172.84	$76,068.00	$62,104.84
Year 9	$143,699.75	$74,598.00	$69,101.75
Year 10	$149,447.74	$73,029.00	$76,418.74
Year 11	$155,425.65	$71,356.00	$84,069.65
Year 12	$161,642.68	$69,570.00	$92,072.68
Year 13	$168,108.38	$67,665.00	$100,443.38
Year 14	$174,832.72	$65,632.00	$109,200.72
Year 15	$181,826.03	$63,463.00	$118,363.03
Year 16	$189,099.07	$61,149.00	$127,950.07
Year 17	$196,663.03	$58,680.00	$137,983.03
Year 18	$204,529.55	$56,045.00	$148,484.55
Year 19	$212,710.73	$53,234.00	$159,476.73
Year 20	$221,219.16	$50,235.00	$170,984.16
Year 21	$230,067.93	$47,035.00	$183,032.93
Year 22	$239,270.65	$43,620.00	$195,650.65
Year 23	$248,841.47	$39,977.00	$208,864.47
Year 24	$258,795.13	$36,090.00	$222,705.13
Year 25	$269,146.94	$31,942.00	$237,204.94
Year 26	$279,912.81	$27,517.00	$252,395.81
Year 27	$291,109.33	$22,795.00	$268,314.33
Year 28	$302,753.70	$17,757.00	$284,996.70
Year 29	$314,863.85	$12,382.00	$302,481.85
Year 30	$327,458.40	$6,647.00	$320,811.40

Note: Appreciation and mortgage reduction is what builds your portfolio over time. Each year the property will realize some appreciation, and each year you will have tenants who are paying down your mortgage balance. Remember, you should be increasing rent annually as well!

We also know that our mortgage balance starts to decrease at a much faster rate after year 10, when you are beginning to pay more toward the principal of the loan. This example is an estimate designed to give you an idea of what your investment portfolio could look like at the end of 30 years. Once again, considering these numbers conservatively, you get the gist of how your portfolio grows!

(*See Appendix 19–Net worth*)

As stated earlier, writing your real estate plan will require some time. This is where you will need to pull information from this book and go through it again, chapter by chapter. Writing your plan will require you not only to evaluate yourself, but also carry out preliminary market research information on the areas in which you are planning to invest. You will need to decide on which investment strategy you are going to use, as well as financing option(s). You will need to ascertain your credit position to determine what your loan-to-value will be, as well as the size of the loan you will qualify for. After completing each of these steps, you will have enough information to formulate your investment plan.

Good luck!

APPENDIX: 2

Credit Reporting Companies

Credit Bureau Contact Information

Equifax	www.equifax.com 1-800-685-1111
Experian	www.experian.com 1-888-397-3742
TransUnion	www.transunion.com 1-800-888-4213

You can also go to www.annualcreditreport.com or call 1-877-322-8228 to request your annual report. This report will provide you a detailed look at all three bureaus and it is usually free if requested once per year.

APPENDIX: 3

Step-By-Step Purchase Transaction

Let's look at a purchase transaction, step-by-step

Buying an investment property from start to finish.

These steps come after you have located a property and are deciding on the best offer to make.

Review Tax Information

I recommend that you use <u>Zillow.com</u> when you are reviewing tax and property value information. Of course, you can always do this the old fashion way by going to the courthouse. You are looking for several things as you review: verification of the owner, the mortgage balance, previous year's taxes and the total assessed market value. Reviewing this information will assist you in formulating your offer.

In this case, say that we learned that the couple selling this property is anxious to sell due to a divorce.

Let's assume the following findings:

Mortgage Balance Information

Transfer (Sale) Information

Based on this tax record, it appears that the owner refinanced the property within the last two years. The original balance of $41,200 was increased to $65,000. Since this loan has not been in place very long, it is safe to assume that the balance is pretty close.

This couple is asking $70,000 for the property. We know that they are looking for a quick sale.

Taxes & Assessments

The total market value includes the land estimate, as well as the property estimate. The total assessed value for the property is $97,000 (the assessed value, in most cases, is usually lower than the appraised value; however, it gives you somewhere to start). Also note that the year market value of the previous year has increased by almost $10,000: the previous year's value of $88,768 has risen to $97,008. This is an indication that the area is appreciating at a rate of 9%!

The Comparative Market Analysis (CMA) shows $105,000 for the property (*See Appendix 5*). This information can also be located online through Zillow, Trulia or out of MLS.

Pre-Qualification

Prior to looking for any investment property, you should have received a pre-qualification status, based on your debt/income ratios, from a bank or mortgage company. From our earlier example, it was determined that you qualified for up to $105,000, 80% loan to value, with a 6.5% interest rate.

Make The Offer

At this point, if you think that it is a good deal and it fits your investment criteria, place the property under contract. Don't forget to write at least one "get-out" clause, in case any of your future findings are not favorable. In this case you can base it on the confirmation of the repair estimate, or a title search.

Writing the contract (See Appendix 8)

Contract amount $70,000

80% LTV

Loan amount of $56,000

APPENDIX: 4

Tax Records

Tax Record

**FULL ASSESSMENT REPORT
COUNTY, USA**

Address: 1234 Highland Drive   Parcel ID: **13187B C010**
Municiplty: Anywhere, US 12345   Land Use: **R RESIDENTIAL**

>>>>LOCATION & OWNERSHIP<<<<

Address:	1234 Highland Drive	District: 13
Prop City/Zip:	Anywhere, US 12345	Land Lot: 4
Owner:	John & Sue Smith	Phone:

>>>>TAXES & ASSESSMENTS<<<<

Market Land Value:	$10,000	Previous Total Tax: $650.00
Market Improved Value:	$87,408	
Total Market Value.	$97,408	Exemptions:
Est. Total Assd Value:	$38,963	
Prior Market Value:	$88,768	Prior Total Tax: $571.29

>>>>TRANSFER (SALE) INFORMATION<<<<
Sale 1 (Recent) Sale 2(Prior)

Sale Date:		
Sale Price:	$79,000	$41,200
Deed Bk/Pg:	3389/280	983/500

MORTGAGE INFORMATION

Amount:	
Date:	Type:
Term:	Rate:
Company: **BANK OF USA**	

>>>>BUILDING CHARACTERISTICS<<<<

Number of Stories:	1.00	Bedrooms:	3
Exterior Walls:	BRICK	Full Baths:	2
Building Style:	RANCH	Half Baths:	0*
Fireplaces:		Total Rooms:	5
Base Sq. Ft:	1,346	Year Built:	
Pool:		Heating:	AIR CONDITION
Pool Type:		Fuel:	
Pool Sq. Ft:	0		
Jacuzzi:		Garage:	GARAGE
		Garage Sq. Ft:	480
		Basement Type:	CRAWL
		Attic Type:	NONE
		Attic Sq. Ft:	

APPENDIX: 5

Comparative Marketing Analysis

Active Single Family Listings									
MLS#	Address	AREA	BR	BAF	BAH	SD	LB	L-PRICE	S
1126622	801 HIGHLAND TERRACE	61	3	1	1	SHERMAN	TBB	$104,000	A
3111560	801 HIGHLAND TERRACE	61	3	2	0	SHERMAN	GLE01	$105,000	A
1226690	729 HIGHLAND PARK	61	3	2	1	SHERMAN	RMAA	$106,900	A
	Listings:	3					Average Listing Price:	$105,000	

MLS#	Address	AREA	BR	BAF	BAH	LB	L-PRICE	S-PRICE	S
1322455	821 HIGHLAND WAY	61	3	1	0	DR1	$103,000	$99,900	S
1280003	780 HIGHLAND PARK	61	3	1	1	MIST09	$105,000	$103,000	S
1303044	765 HIGHLAND DRIVE	61	3	2	0	PRA05	$110,000	$108,000	S
1316928	776 HIGHLAND PARK	61	3	2	0	RMAR	$111,500	$109,000	S
	Listings:	4				Average Listing Price:	$107,575		
						Average Sale Price:	$105,000		

APPENDIX: 6

Cost Estimator

Complete a Cost Estimator form to determine how much will be needed for repairs.

In conjunction with negotiating the contract price, determine the repairs needed for the property. Use the attached Cost Estimator form; tailor one that fits the prices you are actually paying for certain repairs.

*Repairs vary by region; for instance, materials are usually more expensive in the north. Labor might be cheaper, depending on the amount of work available in a particular area. If sub-contractors have a hard time finding work, they will usually work for less money. If work is abundant in an area, the labor rates will be more expensive. Remember to do your home work and always get more than one bid.

This is a very important phase in determining a good deal.

Be sure to over-estimate and add a contingency.

*We have determined that the actual repairs are only $8,000, which is under our $10,000 repairs criteria.

COST ESTIMATOR
1234 HIGHLAND DRIVE

Repairs/Materials Required	Item	Qty	Cost
Interior			
MAJOR COMPONENTS			
Electrical update	$1500-3,000		
Light fixtures	$30-150 per fixture	3	$ 400.00
Plumbing and new fixtures	$300-1,200		
Install central air	$1,500-3,000		
Install new furnace	$1,000-2,000		
KITCHEN			
Kitchen redesign and cabinets	$2,000-4,000		
Ceramic tile in kitchen (floors and countertops)	$600-2,000		
Other			
Appliances	Vary		$ 1,500.00
BATHROOM(S)			
Floors, tub condition, vanity area	$400-1,000		$ 500.00
Tile floors	$3 per sq.		
WALLS - REPAIR ETC...			
Sheetrock work	$100 per wall	4	$ 400.00
Trimwork: labor and materials	$3 per ft.		
Interior painting	$250 per room		
DOORS AND WINDOWS			
Front door	$150-600		$ 200.00
Back door	$150-300		
Window replacement	$100 per window		
Interior doors	$70-100		
FLOORING			
Refinish hardwood floors	$2-4 per sq		
Carpet	$4.00-7.00	200 ft	$ 1,000.00
Carpet cleaning	$25-50 per room		
EXTERIOR			
Replace roof	$1,800-4,500		$ 2,500.00
Gutters	$700-1,200		
Structural leveling			
Concrete	$55 per yard		
Siding/Siding repair			
Exterior painting	$2.00 per sq	300sq	$ 600.00
Elevation enhancements (columnns ralls,etc)			
Security System	$300-500		
Landscaping and grading	$100-500		$ 200.00
10X10 pressure treated lumber deck	$1,200-2,500		
OTHER			
OTHER			
OTHER			
SUBTOTAL			$ 7,300.00
CONTINGENCY	10-20%	10%	$ 730.00
Prices include materials and labor			$ 8,030.00

TOTAL ESTIMATE INCLUDING CONTINGENCY
All prices are estimate, price includes materials and labor

Deal Analysis

Determine whether this is a good deal

The steps for performing the Deal Analysis, once all the information has been gathered are as follows:

Step 1:

You have determined the Estimated Appraised Value, or After Repair Value (ARV), for the property.

Market Research Required:

- ✓ Comparative Market Analysis
- ✓ Tax Information
- ✓ Appraisal information
- ✓ Area rental information

Step 2:

You have determined the repairs needed for the property by using the Cost Estimator form, located in *Appendix 6.*

Step 3:

You have negotiated a deal that fits your strategy and budget.

*Make sure that the property fits your buying plan.

Step 4:

Now you should be able to perform a Deal Analysis on the property to determine whether or not this is a good deal for you.

APPENDIX: 8

Purchase Sale Agreement

THE CONTRACT

If you are purchasing the property directly from the owner, you will need to write your own Purchase Sale Contract. If the property is listed by an agent, or you are working with an agent, then he or she will write it for you to review.

Let's go through it:

Section 1: Purchase and Sale

You will need a full description of the property, which can be obtained from the tax record or the listing sheet for the property. It can also be found on page one of the appraisal.

Section 2: Purchase Price and Method of Payment

Indicate the final agreed-upon terms: the price written out in full, as well as numerically, in US dollars. (Also check the box that applies: obtaining a new loan or paying cash).

It is standard that you make a loan application within 3(three) to 7 (seven) business days of the contract. This should allow you enough time to have the title back if you have not already requested it.

Section 3: Earnest Money

Indicate the holder of the earnest money and the amount (to be paid upon clear title).

Section 4: Closing and Possession

Should clearly outline the date on which the transaction will be closed, as well as the date that the current owner will be out of the property.

Section 5:   Title

This section provides protection for you if the seller cannot "convey good and marketable title by general warranty deed".

Section 6:   Seller's Property Disclosure

This is usually done when a property is listed with a Realtor; however, you can request one to be completed for your information.

Section 7:   Termite Letter

Providing a clearance letter for termites is usually the seller's responsibility. If termites are present, it is also customary for the seller to pay for the treatment cost out of his or her proceeds. Depending on how you structure the contract, this can be your responsibility. (In a lot of states, property cannot be bought or sold without a termite clearance letter.)

Section 8:   Inspection

Most investment property is purchased "as is". However, there are some cases where the seller might ask for certain repairs to be made to a property prior to closing.

Section 9:   Other Provisions

Standard state-specific information to which the contract must adhere.

Section 10:   Disclaimer

Once again, this is standard state-specific information to which the contract must adhere.

Section 11:   Agency and Brokerage

This section can be crossed out if you are writing your own contract. A Realtor would fill this out, if you were using one.

Section 12:   Time Limit of Offer

If you were negotiating by fax or email, as opposed to verbally, you will need to specify a time in which you are allowing the seller to respond. It is extremely important that you control this process, because you want a seller to respond by a given time, especially if you are looking at other property. (The standard is 24-48 hours.)

Section 13:   Exhibits and Addenda

This is where to place any information that overrides the standard contract, such as:

The seller will leave all appliances in the property upon closing. The seller will allow the buyer five business days to check title. The buyer will be responsible for termite clearance. As you can see, this can include anything that both parties agree upon. You can use a separate sheet as well, if you have multiple items.

Bottom Section

Signatures of the Buyer and Seller.

This contract is now ready to be submitted to the lending institution.

Reset the Form

PURCHASE AND SALE AGREEMENT

1   (a) **BUYER NAME(s):** _____

2   (b) **SELLER NAME(s):** _____

3   (c) **PROPERTY ADDRESS and/or DESCRIPTION:** Buyer agrees to purchase and Seller agrees to sell the real property identified as:

4   _____

5   _____, _____ County, Tennessee.

6   (d) **PURCHASE PRICE: $**_____, _____ Dollars,

7   to be paid in cash or equivalent good funds at closing.

8   (e) **EARNEST MONEY: $** _____ valid check or money order payable to Escrow Agent: _____

9   _____, whose address is: _____,

10   will be promptly delivered to Escrow Agent **no later than 5:00 PM, three (3) calendar days after the Acceptance Date.**

11   (f) **CLOSING, EXPIRATION, & POSSESSION DATE:** _____. This is the date that the sale will

12   be closed, or this *Agreement* will expire on this date at 11:59 PM. If this is not a business day, this date will be extended to the

13   next business day. Any other change in this date must be agreed to **in writing** by all parties. Possession of the entire property will

14   be given to the Buyer at the time of closing, unless a different time of possession is agreed to in a separate *Occupancy Agreement.*

15   (g) **ITEMS INCLUDED OR EXCLUDED:** Included, if present, as part of the property sale: all real estate, buildings,

16   improvements, appurtenances (rights and privileges), and fixtures. **Fixtures** include all things which are attached to the

17   structure(s) by nails, screws, or other permanent fasteners, including, but not limited to all of the following, if present:

18   attached light fixtures and bulbs, ceiling fans, attached mirrors; heating and cooling equipment and thermostats; plumbing

19   fixtures and equipment; all doors and storm doors; all windows, screens, and storm windows; all window treatments

20   (draperies, curtains, blinds, shades, etc.) and hardware; all wall-to-wall carpet; all built-in kitchen appliances and stove; all

21   bathroom fixtures; gas logs, fireplace doors and attached screens; all security system components and controls; garage door

22   openers and all remote controls; swimming pool and its equipment; awnings; permanently installed outdoor cooking grills;

23   all fencing, landscaping and outdoor lighting; and mail boxes.

24   Other items included in the sale: _____

25   _____.

26

27   Items that are <u>not</u> included in the sale: _____.

28   Leased items:_____.

29   (h) **CLOSING COSTS:** Unless otherwise stated in Special Stipulations or Addenda, closing costs are to be paid as follows:

30   **Seller must pay** all Seller's existing loans, liens and related costs affecting the sale of the property, Seller's settlement fees,

31   real estate commissions, the balance on any leased items that remain with the property, and a **title insurance policy** with

32   Buyer to receive benefit of simultaneous issue. Any existing rental or lease deposits must be transferred to Buyer at closing.

33   **Buyer must pay** transfer taxes, deed and deed of trust recording fees, association transfer fees, hazard and any other

34   required insurance, Buyer's settlement fees, and **all Buyer's loan related or lender required expenses.**

35   (i) **PRORATIONS, TAXES & ASSESSMENTS:** The current year's property taxes, any existing tenant leases or rents,

36   association or maintenance fees, (and if applicable, any remaining fuel), will be prorated as of the date of closing. Taxes for

37   prior years and any special assessments approved before date of closing must be paid by Seller at or before closing. If

38   applicable, roll back taxes or any tax or assessment that cannot be determined by closing date should be addressed in

39   Special Stipulations or Addenda and will survive the closing.

40   (j) **HOME PROTECTION PLANS:** Home Protection plans available for purchase are **waived, unless** addressed in Special

41   Stipulations. Buyer and Seller understand that an administrative fee may be paid to the Real Estate Company if plan is purchased.

42   (k) **SPECIAL STIPULATIONS:** The following special stipulations, if in conflict with any language contained within the 3 pages of

43   this *Purchase and Sale Agreement*, will control: _____

44   _____

45   _____

46   _____

47   _____

48   _____

49   _____

50   _____.

51   (l) **TIME IS OF THE ESSENCE:** The failure to meet specified time limits will be grounds for canceling this *Agreement.*

52   (m) **FAIR HOUSING AND EQUAL OPPORTUNITY:** This Property is being sold without regard to race, color, sex,

53   religion, disability, marital status, family status, sexual orientation, age, ancestry, or national origin.

Page 1 of 3

54 (n) **FINANCIAL AND APPRAISAL CONTINGENCIES:** This *Agreement* is contingent on Buyer obtaining loan(s) of
55 Buyer's choice. Buyer must deliver to Seller **no later than 5:00 PM, ten (10) calendar days after the Acceptance Date** either
56 documented **proof of available funds** adequate to close, **or** a lender's conditional **commitment letter** proving that: full loan
57 application has been made; the appraisal has been ordered; Buyer's new loan(s) is not contingent on the sale of any other property
58 (unless otherwise stated in this *Agreement*); Buyer has necessary cash reserves; and providing reasonable assurance of Buyer's
59 ability to obtain financing with rates, terms, payments and conditions acceptable to Buyer. Failure to timely provide proof of
60 available funds or commitment letter will be grounds for Seller to cancel this *Agreement* by delivering written *Notice* to Buyer, and all
61 Earnest Money must be refunded to Buyer. *VA/FHA Loan Addendum* must be attached if Buyer is seeking VA or FHA financing.
62 **Appraisal Contingency** - this *Agreement* is also contingent on the appraisal value equaling or exceeding the purchase price.
63 **If any repairs are required by the lender**, Buyer must deliver to Seller a written list of lender required repairs. Seller must
64 deliver to Buyer, no later than 5:00 PM, three (3) calendar days after receiving the repair list, a written *Notice* stating whether or
65 not Seller will complete the repairs before closing at Seller's expense. If Seller does not agree to perform such repairs, or does not
66 reply within the time limit, this *Agreement* will cancel and all Earnest Money must be refunded to Buyer **[see exception in (p)]**.
67 **If, at anytime, the financial or appraisal contingency is not satisfied**, Buyer may cancel this *Agreement* by delivering to
68 Seller a written *Notice of Cancellation*, along with supporting documentation, and all Earnest Money must be refunded to Buyer.

69 (o) **INSPECTION CONTINGENCY AND DUE DILIGENCE PERIOD:** This *Agreement* is contingent on Buyer's
70 satisfaction with all property inspections and investigations. Buyer may use any inspectors of Buyer's choice, at Buyer's
71 expense. Seller must permit Buyer, and Buyer's representatives and inspectors, reasonable access for inspections, with **all
72 utilities in service at Seller's expense.** Buyer assumes all liability for any damage or loss caused by Buyer's or Buyer
73 representatives' inspections or investigations of the property.
74 **Due Diligence Period: All inspections and investigations must be completed with response to Seller no later than
75 5:00 PM, ten (10) calendar days after the Acceptance Date.** *During* this due diligence period Buyer is strongly advised to:
76 (A) have a **professional home inspection** conducted by a licensed home inspector (at Buyer's expense), AND
77 (B) have a **wood destroying insect inspection** conducted by a licensed pest inspector (at Buyer's expense), AND
78 (C) investigate all matters itemized in the *Advisory to Buyers and Sellers* (which is an Addendum to this *Agreement*), AND
79 (D) perform any additional inspections and investigations desired, and verify any other matters of concern to the Buyer, AND
80 (E) if applicable, obtain a septic system inspection letter (available for a fee at TN Dept of Environment and Conservation).
81 **Inspection Contingency Resolution:** If Buyer is satisfied with all inspections and investigations, Buyer may deliver to
82 Seller a *Notice of Release* of inspection contingency. If for **any** reason Buyer is **not** satisfied with the results of **any**
83 inspection or investigation, the Buyer **must**, **within the Due Diligence Period** (Lines 74-75), deliver to Seller **either**:
84 (1) a written *Notice of Cancellation*, canceling this *Agreement*, and all Earnest Money must be refunded to Buyer, **OR**
85 (2) a written *Inspection Contingency Removal Proposal*. If Seller rejects Buyer's *Proposal* (or *Counterproposal*) by delivering
86 a *Notice of Rejection* to Buyer, **or** if any *Counterproposal* is rejected by either party, **or** if a time limit for a written response
87 to such is exceeded, this *Agreement* will cancel and all Earnest Money must be refunded to Buyer **[see exception in (p)]**.
88 - Any *Proposal, Counterproposal, Notice of Rejection,* or *Notice of Release* of inspection contingency must be in writing.
89 - Any *Proposal* or *Counterproposal* must contain a time limit for responding (that is, an expiration date & time).
90 If it is discovered during the Due Diligence Period that any permanent structure on the property has an active wood destroying
91 insect infestation, the Seller, upon Buyer's request, must **professionally treat infestation before closing at Seller's expense.**
92 Repair of any damage from wood destroying insects must be negotiated in the *Inspection Contingency Removal Proposal*.

93 **CAUTION TO BUYER:** Failure to deliver to the Seller either a written *Notice of Release* or *Notice of Cancellation*, or a written
94 *Inspection Contingency Removal Proposal* **within the Due Diligence Period** described on Lines 74-75 will be considered to
95 be an acceptance of the property **"as is,"** and the Inspection Contingency will be satisfied and no longer a part of this *Agreement*.

96 (p) **BUYER'S RIGHT TO REINSTATE:** If Seller refuses to complete the lender required repairs (Lines 63-66), or cancels this
97 *Agreement* by rejecting an *Inspection Contingency Removal Proposal* (Lines 85-89), Buyer has the right to reinstate the
98 *Agreement* by delivering to Seller a *Notice* stating that the Buyer will accept the property in its present "as is" condition. Buyer's
99 *Notice* must be delivered **no later than 5:00 PM, three (3) calendar days after the delivery of Seller's** *Notice* of
100 rejection, or if Seller has failed to respond, no later than 5:00 PM, three (3) calendar days after the Seller's deadline to reply.

101 (q) **FINAL INSPECTION & RISK OF LOSS:** Buyer has the right and responsibility to perform a final inspection before closing
102 to determine that the property is in the same condition, other than ordinary wear, as when the *Agreement* was accepted (with
103 Seller having responsibility to remedy), and to see that any repairs agreed to be performed by Seller have been completed. Buyer
104 may utilize inspectors. All utilities must be in service at Seller's expense. Closing of sale demonstrates acceptance of these items
105 by Buyer. The risk of hazard or casualty loss or damage to the property will be the responsibility of Seller until closing.

106 (r) **DISBURSEMENT OF EARNEST MONEY, AND ADEQUATE CONSIDERATION:** The Earnest Money will be
107 applied towards the purchase price at closing. If any contingencies or conditions of this *Agreement* are not met and the
108 *Agreement* is cancelled, all Earnest Money must be refunded to Buyer. If Seller fails to perform any obligation under this
109 *Agreement*, all Earnest Money must be refunded to Buyer. If required, the Escrow Agent may file an interpleader action in
110 a court of law, and recover expenses and reasonable attorney's fees, and will have no further liability as Escrow Agent. All
111 parties acknowledge that the consideration given, including the promises exchanged, the time limitations imposed, and the
112 notifications required, is sufficient and adequate in exchange for the Buyer's right to legally, properly, and in good faith
113 cancel, reinstate or extend this *Agreement* in accordance with the other terms of this *Agreement*.

Page 2 of 3

114 (s) **TITLE, DEED, & SELLER REPRESENTATIONS:** Seller will convey to Buyer good and marketable title to the property
115 by a valid general warranty deed. Seller, at Seller's expense, agrees to furnish Buyer at closing a title insurance policy. Title
116 policy will be issued by company acceptable to Buyer and Buyer's lender. Buyer will receive benefit of simultaneous issue.
117 **Seller represents** to the best of Seller's knowledge, unless otherwise disclosed, that: **property is not in a Special Flood**
118 **Hazard Area or floodplain;** there are no violations of building, zoning or fire codes; there are no encroachments or
119 violations of setback lines, easements or property boundary lines; and there are no boundary line disputes. If at anytime the
120 title examination, mortgage loan inspection, survey, or other information discloses any such defects, or if the Buyer
121 discovers that any representation in this *Agreement* is in fact untrue, Buyer may, by delivering written *Notice* to Seller,
122 either (1) accept the Property with the defects, OR (2) cancel this *Agreement* and all Earnest Money must be refunded to
123 Buyer, OR (3) Buyer may extend the closing date by up to 3 calendar days to perform additional due diligence, retaining
124 the right to exercise option (1) or (2) above.

125 (t) **DEFAULT OR BREACH:** If either party fails to perform any obligation under this *Agreement*, the other party may do
126 any or all of the following: (1) cancel the *Agreement* (2) sue for specific performance, (3) sue for actual and compensatory
127 damages. Legal counsel is strongly recommended in such circumstances.

128 (u) **REAL ESTATE COMMISSIONS:** Seller authorizes closing company to debit Seller and pay commissions as follows at closing:
129 Real Estate Firm Name: _____will receive_____% of the purchase price.
130 Licensee's Name and Contact Information: _____.
131 Other Real Estate Firm Name (if any): _____will receive_____% of the purchase price.
132 Other Licensee's Name (if any) and Contact Information: _____.

133 (v) **ADDENDA, ATTACHMENTS, EXHIBITS, DISCLAIMERS, AND DISCLOSURES** (included if marked below):
134 ☒ Confirmation of Agency Status (required with **all** Purchase and Sale Agreements)
135 ☒ Advisory to Buyers and Sellers, or TAR Disclaimer Notice (required with **all** Purchase and Sale Agreements)
136 ☐ Lead-Based Paint Disclosure (required for housing **constructed before 1978**)
137 ☐ Personal Interest Disclosure & Consent (required if a **Licensee has a personal interest,** may be included in Confirmation of Agency)
138 ☐ Occupancy Agreement (required if **possession is other than the time of closing**)
139 ☐ VA/FHA Loan Addendum (required if sale involves **VA or FHA financing**)
140 ☐ Impact Fees or Adequate Facilities Taxes Disclosure (required if sale is residential **new construction**)
141 ☐ Subsurface Sewage Disposal System Permit Disclosure (required for newly constructed residential property with **septic system**)
142 ☐ Addendum (extra page for additional Special Stipulations, if needed)
143 ☐ Other: _____
144 *And __one__ of the following three is required with __all__ residential Purchase and Sale Agreements:*
145 ☐ Tennessee Residential Property Condition Disclosure, OR
146 ☐ Tennessee Residential Property Condition Exemption Notification, OR
147 ☐ Tennessee Residential Property Condition Disclaimer Statement

148 (w) **METHOD OF EXECUTION AND DELIVERY:** Signatures and initials transmitted by fax, photocopy, or digital signature
149 methods will be acceptable and treated as originals. This *Agreement* constitutes the sole and entire agreement between the
150 parties. No verbal agreements, representations, promises, or modifications of this *Agreement* will be binding unless agreed
151 to in writing by all parties. **Delivery** will be considered to have been completed as of the date and time a document is either
152 (1) delivered in person, OR (2) transmitted by fax, OR (3) transmitted by email. Delivery of documents to the real estate Licensee
153 assisting a party as that party's agent or facilitator (or to that Licensee's Broker) will be considered to be Delivery to that party.

154 (x) **ACCEPTANCE DATE AND BINDING CONTRACT:** The **Acceptance Date** will be the date of full execution (signing) of this
155 *Agreement* by all parties, that is, the date one party accepts all the terms of the other party's written and signed *Offer* or *Counteroffer*,
156 evidenced by the accepting party's signature and date on the *Offer* or *Counteroffer*. The Acceptance must be promptly
157 communicated (by any reasonable and usual mode) to the other party, thereby making this *Agreement* a legally **Binding Contract**.
158 Communications to the real estate Licensee assisting a party as that party's agent or facilitator (or to that Licensee's Broker) will
159 be considered to be communication to that party. True executed copies of the Contract must be promptly delivered to all parties.

160 (y) **OFFER EXPIRATION DATE & TIME:** _____. If not Accepted by
161 this date & time (or if blank, by the date and time on Lines 11-13), this *Offer* will expire. However, at any time before the
162 other party's communication of Acceptance, the party making the *Offer* may **withdraw** the *Offer* by communicating the
163 withdrawal to the other party, and confirm the withdrawal by the prompt delivery of a written *Notice of Withdrawal*.

164 **Buyer makes this *Offer*.**

165 X_____   X_____
     Buyer Signature   *Date & Time*   *Buyer Signature*   *Date & Time*

166 **This *Offer* is:** ☐ **Accepted**   ☐ **Rejected**   ☐ **Countered on this form**   ☐ **Countered on a separate *Counteroffer* form**

167 X_____   X_____
     Seller Signature   *Date & Time*   *Seller Signature*   *Date & Time*

APPENDIX: 9

Reviewing an Appraisal

Five key things to look for when reviewing any appraisal:

1.   **Neighborhood**

It is important to note whether the appraiser is listing any adverse information about the neighborhood that may cause you to re-think your investment. This information is located on page one of the appraisal, under NEIGHBORHOOD.

2.   **Square Footage**

This is important because values are derived based on square footage. It is good to know what the price per square foot is in a particular area, for future re-sells or investment purposes.

This information is located on page 1 of the appraisal, under DESCRIPTION OF IMPROVEMENTS.

3.   **Value**

Normally, you will see three approaches on an investment property appraisal (depends on lender requirements).

Cost Approach

Determines the cost if the property were to be rebuilt from the ground.

Sales Approach

This is the value of the property if it were sold on the market. This approach compares like property in the area in order to come up with the sales value.

Income Approach

This approach takes into account the Estimated Market Rent of the property, based on the amount that "like" property in the area will rent for; it derives a value. This also gives you, as the investor, an idea of what the property can rent for; however, you should have contacted your appraiser before now, during the market research phase.

All of this information is located on page 2 of the appraisal, under SALES COMPARISON ANALYSIS.

4. **Sales Comparison**

   This section compares a minimum of three properties, which are similar in size, build and quality to the subject property. Become familiar with the actual properties listed here; they are definite indications of the value of the property that you are purchasing.

   Properties are compared based on: site, design, quality, age, condition, room count and square footage, basements, porches, garages, fencing, and other extras that the property may have which give it additional value.

   Note: Normally, if the value of the property cannot be verified, the Appraiser will notify you immediately.

5. **Supplemental Addendum Page or Appraiser Comments**

   Pay close attention to this page, because the lender definitely reviews it! Basically, it gives an overview of the *Appendix 9* appraisal and points out concerns that he or she may have. Remember, at this point the lender is relying on the appraiser to determine the value of the property. This is the lender's collateral if you default!

   The remainder of the appraisal consists of pictures, maps and layouts.

Submit Contract To Lending Institution

Upon submitting the contract, an appraisal will have to be ordered to accompany the loan package to the lender.

Loan Package

❑ Executed contract (fully signed by all parties)

❑ Copy of the appraisal, verifying value of at least the contract price

❑ Copy of all signed state disclosures, including the Good Faith Estimate and Truth In Lending

APPENDIX: 10

Good Faith Estimate Truth in Lending Estimate

Let's review the Good Faith Estimate and Truth In Lending documents associated with the loan. We have submitted the contract for the amount of $56,000, 80% LTV, $2,000 closing cost being paid by seller, with an interest rate of 6.5%.

Note: The charges listed on the Good Faith Estimate can vary from state to state and from lending institution to lending institution. This is an example only, used to enable you to become familiar with the document. These are both considered universal documents.

Reviewing The Good Faith Estimate (GFE):

Lines 800-812

Deal with fees associated with the lending institution: this is what the lender is charging to close the loan. Most of these fees are set based on the institution; however, find out if some type of discount can be applied if you are planning to purchase multiple properties.

Lines 1100-1108

Deal with Title Charges and Attorney fees. In most states, an attorney must close all real estate transactions. However, in the states that this is not the case, you should still be provided with a Good Faith Estimate.

Lines 1200-1203

Recording fees and transfer charges (state-specific).

Line 1300

Reflects any additional settlement charges that you have agreed to pay, according to the contract.

This provides the total estimated closing costs; in this case, $2,610.00.

The next section of the Good Faith Estimate deals with items that are paid in advance. Your broker should be able to inform you of these charges and whether or not the seller can pay any of them. Some lenders require that the buyer be responsible for pre-paid items.

Lines 900-905

Interest charges, mortgage insurance and hazard (property) insurance.

Line 1000-1005

This section is only required if you are setting up an escrow account to pay your taxes and insurance. Depending on the individual, you can decide whether you want to be responsible for your own taxes and insurance. Based on the loan program type, the lender might require that you have an escrow account. Appendix 10

(If you have limited time to track your investments, I would suggest that you set up an escrow. This way you won't have to try and remember when these items come due.)

The bottom section of the GFE recaps the total purchase price, applying the closing costs to be paid by the seller, which gives you the balance of the closing cost plus your 20% down.

In this transaction 20% down ($14,000), then adding the total closing costs of $2,733.33, brings the total to $17,243.33 that we need, less the $2,000 being contributed by the seller. The final number reflected at the bottom of the GFE is $15,733.33. Monthly payment, including escrow, total $463.00.

If you can live with these numbers, then you are on your way! If you can't, go back to the drawing board real fast.

Reviewing The Truth In Lending (TIL)

Now let's take a look at the Truth in Lending document associated with this purchase. The thing to remember here is that the interest rate may appear to be higher because it is taking into account the financing of the closing cost. The finance charge associated with this loan will be $71,423.00; this is how much interest you will pay over the life of the loan.

"**Amount financed**" is the amount that you are financing: $56,000.00.

"**Total of payments**": If you keep this loan for the full 30-year term, you will have paid a total of $127,423.00!

This document also discloses the number of payments that you will make, and takes into account principal and interest only.

Also, look at the bottom of this document to make sure nothing is checked that you are not agreeing to.

*Looking at this disclosure further confirms why you would want to pay the loan off fairly quickly, to cut the amount of interest you will have to pay. As an investor the good part is that all or most of the interest is a write-off to you!

The Truth-in-Lending Act is aimed at promoting the informed use of consumer credit by requiring disclosures about terms and costs.

SAMPLE TRUTH-IN-LENDING DISCLOSURE STATEMENT
(THIS IS NEITHER A CONTRACT NOR A COMMITMENT TO LEND)

Applicants:
Property Address:
Application No:

Because you may be paying points and other fees, the APR disclosed is often higher than the interest rate on your loan. The APR can be compared to other loans to give you a fair method of comparing prices.

Prepared By:

Date Prepared:

The mortgage amount minus prepaid finance charges (loan origination fees, points, adjusted interest and initial mortgage insurance premium) and any required balance. It represents a net figure to allow you to accurately assess the amount of credit actually provided.

ANNUAL PERCENTAGE RATE	FINANCE CHARGE	AMOUNT FINANCED	TOTAL OF PAYMENTS	
The cost of your credit as a yearly rate	The dollar amount the credit will cost you	The amount of credit provided to you or on your behalf	The amount you will have paid after making all payments as scheduled	*The estimated total amount you will have paid, including principal, interest, prepaid finance charges and mortgage insurance, if you make minimum payments for the entire loan term.*
6.5 %	$ 71,423	$ 56,000	$ 127,423	

REQUIRED DEPOSIT: The annual percentage rate does not take into account your required deposit

PAYMENTS: Your payment schedule will be:

Number of Payments	Amount of Payments**	When Payments Are Due	Number of Payments	Amount of Payments**	When Payments Are Due	Number of Payments	Amount of Payments**	When Payments Are Due
		Monthly Beginning:			Monthly Beginning:			Monthly Beginning:

Principal, interest and mortgage insurance if applicable.

The estimated total amount of interest payments for the term of the loan, the amount of interest paid at closing, origination fee and any other charges paid to the lender.

Defines circumstances under which the remaining principal and interest amount of the loan is due and payable on demand.

DEMAND FEATURE: This obligation has a demand feature.

VARIABLE RATE FEATURE: This loan has a variable rate feature. A variable rate disclosure has been provided earlier.

CREDIT LIFE/CREDIT DISABILITY: Credit life insurance and credit disability insurance are not required to obtain credit, and will not be provided unless you sign and agree to pay the additional cost.

Type	Premium	Signature	
Credit Life		I want credit life insurance.	Signature:
Credit Disability		I want credit disability insurance.	Signature:
Credit Life and Disability		I want credit life and disability insurance.	Signature:

INSURANCE: The following insurance is required to obtain credit:

   Credit life insurance   Credit disability   Property insurance   Flood insurance

You may obtain the insurance from anyone you want that is acceptable to creditor

   If you purchase   property   flood insurance from creditor you will pay $ for a one year term.

SECURITY: You are giving a security interest in:

   The goods or property being purchased   Real property you already own

FILING FEES: $ *An estimate of the cost of recording the legal documents (mortgage or deed of trust) connected with the transaction, which will be charged at closing.*

LATE CHARGE: If a payment is more than   days late, you will be charged   % of the payment

Defines whether a fee will be charged and if you would be eligible for a refund if you wish to repay part or all of the loan in advance of the regular schedule. If you are not entitled to a refund, you will be charged interest for the period of time you used the money loaned to you. Your prepaid finance charges and any interest already paid are generally not refundable. If you pay the loan off early, you should not have to pay the full amount of the finance charges shown on the disclosure.

PREPAYMENT: If you pay off early, you

   may   will not   have to pay a penalty.

   may   will not   be entitled to a refund of part of the finance charge.

Defines whether or not the loan can be passed on from a seller of a home to another buyer, where the buyer "assumes" all outstanding payments.

ASSUMPTION: Someone buying your property

   may   may, subject to condition   may not   assume the remainder of your loan on the original terms.

See your contract documents for any additional information about nonpayment, default, any required repayment in full before the scheduled date and prepayment refunds and penalties.

** NOTE: The Payments shown above include reserve deposits for mortgage insurance (if applicable), but exclude property taxes and insurance.

THE UNDERSIGNED ACKNOWLEDGES RECEIVING A COMPLETED COPY OF THIS DISCLOURE.

_____
(Applicant)   (Date)

_____
(Lender)   (Date)

Lenders are required by law to provide the information on this statement in a timely manner. Your signature merely indicates that you received this information and does not obligate you or the lender in any way.

The Real Estate Settlement Procedures Act (RESPA) is designed to inform consumers when shopping for a mortgage loan by disclosing the estimated costs associated with obtaining the loan.

➤ **SAMPLE GOOD FAITH ESTIMATE**

Applicants:
Property Address:
Prepared By:

Application No:
Date Prepared:
Loan Program:

The information provided below reflects estimates of the charges that you are likely to incur at the settlement of your loan. The fees listed are estimates - actual charges may be more or less. Your transaction may not involve a fee for every item listed. The numbers listed beside the estimates generally correspond to the numbered lines contained in the HUD-1 settlement statement, which you will be receiving at settlement. The HUD-1 settlement statement will show you the actual cost for items paid at settlement.

Total Loan Amount $ 56,000   Interest Rate: 6.5 %   Term: 30 mths 360

800	ITEMS PAYABLE IN CONNECTION WITH LOAN:			PFC S F POC
801	Loan Origination Fee		$ 560.00	
802	Loan Discount			
803	Appraisal Fee			
804	Credit Report		300.00	PFC= Prepaid Finance Charge
805	Lender's Inspection Fee			(fees that affect the APR)
808	Mortgage Broker Fee			S= Seller Paid
809	Tax Related Service Fee			F= FHA Allowable Fees
810	Processing Fee			POC= Paid Outside of Closing
811	Underwriting Fee	Underwriting and Processing combined	750.00	
812	Wire Transfer Fee			
1100	TITLE CHARGES:			PFC S F POC
1101	Closing or Escrow Fee:		$	
1105	Document Preparation Fee		100.00	
1106	Notary Fees			
1107	Attorney Fees			
1108	Title Insurance:	Understand this charge	700.00	
1200	GOVERNMENT RECORDING & TRANSFER CHARGES:			PFC S F POC
1201	Recording Fees:		$	
1202	City/County Tax/Stamps:		100.00	
1203	State Tax/Stamps:		100.00	
1300	ADDITIONAL SETTLEMENT CHARGES:			PFC S F POC
1302	Pest Inspection		$	
		Estimated Closing Costs	2,610.00	
900	ITEMS REQUIRED BY LENDER TO BE PAID IN ADVANCE:			PFC S F POC
901	Interest for 30 days @ $ 10.11 per day		$ 303.33	
902	Mortgage Insurance Premium		*Elements of your projected loan payments (interest,*	
903	Hazard Insurance Premium		*taxes and insurance) that must be prepaid to*	
904			*establish the escrow account and the loan schedule.*	
905	VA Funding Fee			
1000	RESERVES DEPOSITED WITH LENDER:			PFC S F POC
1001	Hazard Insurance Premium 3 months @ $ 40.00 per month		$ 120.00	
1002	Mortgage Ins. Premium Reserves months @ $ per month			
1003	School Tax months @ $ per month			
1004	Taxes and Assessment Reserves 3 months @ $ 70.00 per month		210.00	
1005	Flood Insurance Reserves months @ $ per month			
		Estimated Prepaid Items/Reserves	633.33	

TOTAL ESTIMATED SETTLEMENT CHARGES $ 3,243.33   S ($2,000)

TOTAL ESTIMATED FUNDS NEEDED TO CLOSE:		TOTAL ESTIMATED MONTLY PAYMENT:	
Purchase Price/Payoff (+)	70,000	New First Mortgage (-)	Principal & Interest 353.00
Loan Amount (-)	56,000	Sub Financing (-)	Other Financing (P & I)
Est. Closing Costs (+)	2,610.00	New 2nd Mtg Closing Costs (+)	Hazard Insurance 40.00
Est. Prepaid Items/Reserves (+)	633.33		Real Estate Taxes 70.00
Amount Paid by Seller (-)	2,000.00		Mortgage Insurance
			Homeowner Assn. Dues
			Other
Total Est. Funds needed to close 15,243.33		**Total Monthly Payment** 463.00	

These estimates are provided pursuant to the Real Estate Settlement Procedures Act of 1974, as amended (RESPA). Additional information can be found in the HUD Special Information Booklet, which is to be provided to you by your mortgage broker or lender, if your application is to purchase residential real estate property and the lender will take a first lien on the property. The undersigned acknowledges receipt of the booklet "Settlement Costs," and if applicable the Consumer Handbook on ARM Mortgages

Applicant   Date   Applicant   Date

Partnership Agreements

You can tailor a Joint Venture Contract to fit your specified partnering terms. This is recommended, as it is definitely advantageous to have a contract in place, no matter how well you know your partner. It is also good to have as a point of reference and in case a partner dies; the contract specifies the terms for the deceased member's survivors.

If you don't feel comfortable putting together your own agreement, you can contact a real estate attorney and he/she can put one together for you. It is important to have your documents notarized.

JOINT VENTURE AGREEMENT

THIS JOINT VENTURE AGREEMENT (the "Agreement") made and entered into as of this _____day of _____(year), by and between _____ and _____.

ARTICLE I
GENERAL PROVISIONS

Business Purpose. The business of the Joint Venture shall be as follows:

List specific details regarding the transaction. Should include address, investments amount, expected profits, how profits are to divided and overall purpose of the partnership.

Term of the Agreement. This Joint Venture shall commence on the date first above written and shall continue in existence until terminated, liquidated, or dissolved by law or as hereinafter provided.

ARTICLE II
GENERAL DEFINITIONS

The following comprise the general definitions of terms utilized in this Agreement:

2.01 Affiliate. An Affiliate of an entity is a person that, directly or indirectly through one or more intermediaries, controls, is controlled by or is under common control of such entity.

Capital Contribution(s). The capital contribution to the Joint Venture actually made by the parties, including property, cash and any additional capital contributions made.

Profits and Losses. Any income or loss of the Partnership for federal income tax purposes determined by the Partnership's fiscal year _____including, without limitation, each item of Partnership income, gain, loss or deduction.

ARTICLE III
OBLIGATIONS OF THE JOINT VENTURE

Duties of each partner should be defined in this section.

ARTICLE IV
PROFIT AND LOSSES

Profits and Losses. Commencing on the date hereof and ending on the termination of the business of the Joint Venture, all profits, losses and other allocations to the Joint Venture shall be allocated as follows as the conclusion of the venture.

Partner 1   Net Profit 50%
Partner 2   Net Profit 50%

ARTICLE V
RIGHTS AND DUTIES OF THE JOINT VENTURE

Business of the Joint Venture. <u>Partner 1</u> shall have full, exclusive and complete authority in the management and control of the business of the Joint Venture for the purposes herein stated and shall make all decisions affecting the business of the Joint Venture. At such, any action taken shall constitute the act of, and serve to bind, the Joint Venture.

<u>Partner 2</u> shall manage and control the affairs of the Joint Venture to the best of its ability and shall use its best efforts to carry out the business of the Joint Venture, <u>Partner 2</u> shall have limited control over the Joint Venture business and shall not participate in or have any control over the Joint Venture business nor shall it have any authority or right to act for or bind the Joint Venture.

(Specify language that applies to the rights and duties of your Joint Venture)

ARTICLE VI
AGREEMENTS WITH THIRD PARTIES AND WITH
AFFILIATES OF THE JOINT VENTURE

Validity of Transactions. Affiliates of the parties to this Agreement may be engaged to perform services for the Joint Venture. Services such as (   ) where applicable. Affiliates of the parties to this Agreement otherwise permitted by the terms of this Agreement shall not be affected by reason of the relationship between them and such Affiliates or the approval of said transactions, agreement or payment.

(Tailor to fit affiliations that the joint venture may be subject to)

6.02 Other Business of the Parties to this Agreement. The parties of this Agreement and their respective Affiliates may have interests in businesses other than the Joint Venture business. The Joint Venture shall not have the right to the income or proceeds from such other business interests and, even if they are competitive with the Partnership business, such business interests shall not be deemed wrongful or improper.

ARTICLE VII
PAYMENT OF EXPENSES

All unforeseen expenses of the Joint Venture shall be paid by both parties and shall be reimbursed by the Joint Venture.

ARTICLE VIII
INDEMNIFICATION OF THE JOINT VENTURES

The parties to this Agreement shall have no liability to the other for any loss suffered which arises out of any action or inaction if, in good faith, it is determined that such course of conduct was in the best interests of the Joint Venture and such course of conduct did not constitute negligence or misconduct. The parties of this Agreement shall each be indemnified by the other against losses, judgments, liabilities, expenses, and amounts paid in settlement of any claims sustained by it in connection with the Joint Venture.

ARTICLE IX
DISSOLUTION

9.01 Events of the Joint Venture. The Joint Venture shall be dissolved upon the happening of any of the following events:

(a) The adjudication of bankruptcy, filing of a petition pursuant to a Chapter of the Federal Bankruptcy Act, withdrawal, removal or insolvency of either of the parties.

The sale or other disposition, not including an exchange of all, or substantially all, of the Joint Venture assets.

Mutual agreement of the parties.

IN WITNESS WHEREOF, the parties hereto have executed this Agreement as of the day and year first above written.

Signature of Parties:

_____
Date

_____
Date

Notary Public

_____
Date

APPENDIX: 12

Quitclaim Deed

Legal document to transfer property rights

QUITCLAIM DEED

STATE OF_____ COUNTY OF _____

This Indenture made this _____day of _____in the year _____ between New Owner/Grantee of FULTON County, Georgia, as party or parties of the first part, hereinunder called Grantor, and **Existing Owner/Grantor** as party or parties of the second part, hereinafter called Grantee (the words "Grantor" and "Grantee" to include their respective heirs, successors and assigns where the context requires or permits)

WITNESSETH that: Grantor, for and in consideration of the sum of _____ ($) and other good and valuable considerations in hand paid at and before the sealing and delivery of these presents, the receipt whereof is hereby acknowledged, has bargained, sold, and does by these presents bargain, sell, remise, release and forever QUIT-CLAIM to Grantee all the right, title interest claim or demand which Grantor has or may have in and to:

See Exhibit A attached hereto and made a part hereof.

TO HAVE AND TO HOLD the said described premises unto Grantee so that neither Grantor nor any other person or persons claiming under Grantor shall at any time, claim or demand any right, title or interest to the aforesaid described premises or its appurtenances.

IN WITNESS WHEREOF, Grantor has hereunto set grantors hand and seal this day and year first above written.

Signed, sealed and delivered in the Presence of:

_____

Witness

_____

Grantee   Notary

_____

Grantor

EXHIBIT "A"

ALL THAT TRACT OR PARCEL OF LAND LYING AND BEING
IN LAND LOT 100 OF THE 10TH DISTRICT OF ANYWHERE
COUNTY, BEING LOT 850, CAPITOL SUBDIVISION, AS PER PLAT
RECORDED IN PLAT BOOK 3, PAGE 113, ANYWHERE COUNTY
RECORDS, WHICH PLAT IS INCORPORATED HEREIN BY THIS
REFERENCE AND MADE A PART OF THIS DESCRIPTION.

(A complete legal description must accompany the filing).

APPENDIX: 13

Sample postcards

QUICK CASH
For Your Property!

- ✓ Relocating
- ✓ Job Loss
- ✓ Facing Foreclosure
- ✓ Debt Relief

We can help!

Contact Bob at 555-1234

I
BUY
HOUSES
Call 555-1234
24 hours a day

APPENDIX: 14

Contractor's contract

CONTRACT FOR SERVICES

For the property having the address _____

Contractor agrees to perform the labor with supplying all materials except as noted herein for the herein described work in a workman-like manner for a fee of $8,000.00 (Amount). Contractor agrees not to pull off job until job is completed and accepted by manager. If contractor should pull off the job, or cease work for any reason prior to completion, all monies due shall become null and void. Job will be completed and accepted by manager no later than 6:00 p.m. Date or $75.00 per day penalty, including weekend days, may be charged to balance due contractor. The owner will provide all materials. Contractor states that he does have all necessary licenses, permits, and insurance overages necessary to legally perform herein described work and does aggress to hold owner harmless from any and all claims arising from same, and to waive the right to lien the property for any and all reasons. Contractor further agrees that all workers hired by contractor shall look to him, the contractor, for all payments due for work.

Materials, debris, and/or junk are not to be piled in the yard. (It may be neatly placed on curb). Any materials, debris, or junk left in the yard for more than 48 hours will be hauled away by the owner/manager. Hauling fees and landscape repairs will be back charged to the contractor. Contractor or their employees will not park or drive in the yard at any time. The contractor will be back charged for all landscape repairs for damages during the time on the job site.

The contractor agrees that he shall remedy any defects Real Estate and Wealth resulting from faulty workmanship that shall become evident during a period of <u>ONE YEAR</u> after completion of the work.

The provision shall apply with equal force to all work performed by subcontractors and laborers as well as to work that is performed directly by the contractor himself.

The Contract Price shall be paid to the contractor in the following manner: EIGHT-THOUSAND DOLLARS AFTER COMPLETION AND INSPECTION.

Work performed: *Specify details here.*

Manager/Owner _____

Date _____

Contractor _____

Date _____

Social Security/Tax Identification

_____

Hold Harmless Clause:
Contractor agrees not to hold Owner responsible for any mishaps/ injuries that may occur on the property site.

_____ Contractor

*Note: License and insurance should be provided and attached to executed contract.

APPENDIX: 15

Settlement Statement

This is the final stage of the loan process. Your lending institution should contact you 24 hours prior to closing, in order to cover what is referred to as the Settlement Statement, or HUD. This should outline for you the exact cost associated with the loan. On your side (buyer), this document should mirror the Good Faith Estimate that you received when you originally applied for the loan. As stated in Chapter 8, during the loan process each time your bottom line changes by $250.00, you should be provided with a new GFE.

At this point, in most cases, you will have to bring certified funds to the closing.

Congratulations! You have closed your first investment deal!

APPENDIX: 16

Sample Lease

RENTAL AGREEMENT

DATE:

PROPERTY ADDRESS:

MANAGEMENT:

RESIDENTS:

APPLIANCES:

INITIAL TERM: 12 MONTHS

BEGINNING DATE:

TERMINATION DATE:

MONTHLY RENTAL:

SECURITY DEPOSIT:

Attached hereto is the sole and entire rental agreement between the aforementioned management and resident, and both parties acknowledge receipt of completed copies. No oral statements shall be binding. No modification of this agreement shall be binding unless attached hereto and signed by all parties. When so indicated above, all parties acknowledge that management is a licensed real estate broker. Management represents the owner of the subject property, and will be compensated by the owner for professional services rendered. In witness whereof, the parties hereto have caused these presents to be signed in person or by a person duly authorized, the day and year above written.

RENTAL AGREEMENT

In consideration of the mutual covenants herein set forth, Resident leases from Management, and Management leases to Resident the dwelling located at the aforementioned Property Address (hereinafter referred to as "the premises") for the period commencing at noon on the aforementioned Beginning Date, and monthly thereafter until noon on the aforementioned Termination Date, at which time this Agreement is terminated. Resident, in consideration of Management permitting them to occupy the premises, hereby agrees to the following terms:

1. **RENT:** Rent shall be the aforementioned "Monthly Rental" per month, payable in full and in advance, without notice or demand, upon the 5th day of each calendar month to Management at the address specified as "Address of Management", or at such other place as may be designated by Management from time to time. Rent checks received in advance will be deposited only on the due date.

2. **DISCOUNT RENT:** *N/A (Can be given to encourage timely rental payments, i.e. by the 1st of each month, $20.00 off)*

3. **LATE FEES:** *Time is of the essence.* If the rent is not paid by the fifth day of the month, Resident shall pay a penalty of $50.00 to Management, and Resident shall pay a further penalty of $10.00 per day thereafter until the rent is paid to Management as additional rent, due and payable each day. Each daily failure to pay such additional rent shall be a separate event of default. In the event any check given by Resident to Management is returned by the bank unpaid, Resident shall pay a $50.00 return check fee to Management as additional rent in addition to the aforementioned daily late fees, with all subsequent payments thereafter due and payable in certified funds.

4. **UTILITIES:** Resident shall be responsible for the payment of all utilities and services, and agrees to maintain and pay for electric, gas and water service at the residence during the entire term of this agreement. Disconnection of utility services at dwelling prior

to termination date shall constitute an event of default under this agreement.

5. **USE:** The premises shall be used solely as a residence and shall be occupied only by persons named as the aforementioned RESIDENTS in this Agreement. Occupancy by guests staying over seven days will be in violation of this provision. No pets of any kind shall be brought on the premises without the prior written consent of the Management. Resident shall not have a waterbed on the premises without prior written consent of the Management. Resident shall comply with the laws, ordinances, restrictions, and regulations of any relevant governmental body. Resident shall not use the premises or permit it to be used for any unlawful purpose including, but not limited to, use, sale, possession, or distribution of illegal drugs or any other violations of any law regarding controlled substances. Such activity on the premises shall constitute an event of default under the Agreement and Management may, at its option, terminate this agreement and resident shall be subject to immediate eviction. Management, upon suspicion of such illegal activity, shall immediately notify and cooperate with the appropriate authorities, and any such action by Management shall not be construed as an invasion of resident's privacy. Resident waives any claim for trespass, defamation, or invasion of privacy against Management when Management is cooperating with police or other duly constituted authorities.

6. **MAINTENANCE, REPAIRS OR ALTERATIONS:** Resident acknowledges that the premises are in good order and repair, and resident accepts the premises "as is", unless otherwise indicated herein. Resident shall at his own expense, and at all times, maintain the premises in a clean and sanitary manner including all equipment, appliances, furniture and furnishings therein and shall surrender the same, at termination hereof, in as good condition as received, normal wear and tear excepted. Resident shall be responsible for damages caused by his negligence and that of his family, or invitees, or guests. Resident shall not paint, paper or otherwise redecorate or make alterations to the premises

without the prior written consent of the Management. Resident shall mow, irrigate and maintain the grounds of the premises, including lawns and shrubbery and gutters, and keep the same clear of rubbish, weeds, or leaves if such grounds are a part of the premises and are available for the use of the Resident. In the event that Resident fails to maintain lawns or shrubbery which are a part of premises, Management, after attempting to notify Resident, may, but is not required to, maintain lawns and/or shrubbery by using a professional yard maintenance company. The Resident will pay the costs of any such yard maintenance.

7. **RIGHT OF ACCESS:** Management may enter the premises without notice for inspection, repairs and maintenance during reasonable hours. In case of emergency, management may enter at any time to protect life and/or prevent damage. During the last sixty days of the term hereof and during reasonable hours, Management may display the interior and exterior of dwelling at premises to any prospective tenants or purchasers, and Resident agrees to provide access thereto.

8. **INDEMNIFICATION:** Management shall not be liable for any damage or injury to the Resident, or any other person, or to any property, occurring on the premises, or any part thereof, or in common areas thereof, unless such damage is the proximate result of the gross negligence or unlawful act of the Management, his agents, or his employees. Resident does hereby indemnify, release, and save harmless management and management's agents from and against any and all suits, actions, claims, judgments, and expenses arising out of or relating to any loss of life, bodily or personal injury, property damage, or other demand, claim or action of any nature arising out of or related to this lease or the use of this premises. Further and in addition, Resident releases Management from liability for, and agrees to indemnify Management against all losses incurred by Management as a result of Resident's failure to fulfill any condition of this lease; any damage or injury happening in or about the premises to Resident or Resident's guests, invitees, or licensees or such persons' property, except where such damage

or injury is due to gross negligence or willful misconduct of Management; Resident's failure to comply with any requirements imposed by any governmental authority; and any judgment, lien, or other encumbrance filed against the premises as a result of Resident's actions.

9. **ESCALATION CLAUSE:** The Management shall reserve the right to increase the rent during the term of this lease upon a 60 day written notice to the resident. The Resident shall approve or reject this proposal in writing within seven days of receipt. Upon rejection, the Management may, at its option, cause the Termination Date to be accelerated to a date not less than 60 days following the date of rejection as stated in writing. (Not commonly used any more, but if you are ever in a situation where rental property is hard to find, you may want to consider something like this)

10. **POSSESSION:** If, for any reason, Management is unable to deliver possession of the premises at the commencement hereof, Management shall not be liable for any damages caused thereby, nor shall this agreement be void or void able, but Resident shall not be liable for any rent until possession is delivered. Resident may terminate this agreement if possession is not delivered within seven (7) days of the commencement of the term hereof.

11. **DEFAULT:** If Resident shall fail to pay rent when due, or fail to perform any term or condition of this agreement, including, but not limited to, failure to reimburse Management for any damages, repairs, or costs when due, then Management, at its option, may terminate all rights of Resident hereunder, unless Resident, within two days after notice thereof, shall cure such default. If Resident abandons or vacates the premises, while in default of the payment of rent, Management may consider any property left on the premises to be abandoned and may dispose of the same in any manner allowed by law, without responsibility or liability therefore. In the event the Management reasonably believes that such abandoned property has no value, it may be discarded. All property on the premises is hereby subject to a lien in favor of Management for

payment of all sums due hereunder, to the maximum extent allowed by law. In the event of a default by Resident, Management may elect to (a) continue the lease in effect and enforce all his rights and remedies hereunder, including the right to recover the rent as it comes due, or (b) at any time, terminate all of Resident's rights hereunder and recover from Resident all damages Management may incur by reason of the breach of the lease, including the cost of recovering the premises, and including the worth at the time of such termination, or at the time of an award if suit be instituted to enforce this provision, of the amount by which the unpaid rent for the balance of the term exceeds the amount of such rental loss which the Resident proves could be reasonably avoided.

12. **DAMAGE TO THE PREMISES:** If the premises are totally destroyed or so substantially damaged by storm, fire, earthquake, flooding, or other casualty as to be rendered untenantable, this lease shall terminate as of the date of such destruction or damage, and rental shall be accounted for between management and resident as of that date. If the leased premises should be damaged (but not rendered wholly untenantable) to the extent that management shall decide not to rebuild or repair, the term of this lease shall end and the rent shall be prorated up to the time of the damage.

13. **SECURITY:** The security deposit set forth, if any, shall secure the performance of Resident's obligations hereunder. Management may, but shall not be obligated to, apply all or portions of said deposit on account of Resident's obligations hereunder, and may, but are not obligated to, maintain such funds in an interest bearing account. Any interest accruing shall become the property of Management or Agent for Management. Resident shall not apply the Security Deposit in payment of the last month's rent, unless the Management has given prior written consent. Nothing in this agreement shall preclude the Management from retaining the security deposit for nonpayment of rent or of fees, for abandonment of the premises (abandonment fee shall be equal to one month's rent), for nonpayment of utility charges, for repair work or cleaning contracted for by the resident with third parties,

for unpaid pet fees, or for actual damages caused by the resident's breach. Resident specifically acknowledges receipt of the MOVE-IN INSPECTION LIST prior to the tendering of any security deposit.

14. **ASSIGNMENT AND SUBLETTING:** Resident may not sublet dwelling or assigns this lease without the written consent of Management.

15. **ATTORNEY'S FEES:** In any legal action to enforce the terms hereof or relating to the demised premises, the prevailing party shall be entitled to all costs incurred in connection with such action, including a reasonable attorney's fee, plus all costs of collection.

16. **WAIVER:** No failure of Management to enforce any term hereof shall be deemed a waiver, nor shall any acceptance of a partial payment of rent (or any payment marked "payment in full") be deemed a waiver of Management's right to the full amount thereof. No term, covenant or condition of this agreement may be waived by Management unless such waiver is in writing and signed by Management

17. **NOTICE:** Any notice which either party may or is required to give, shall be in writing and delivered either (1) in person, or (2) by mailing the same, first class postage paid, to Resident at the premises, or to Management at address specified as "Address of Management", or at such other places as may be designated in writing by the parties from time to time. Management is authorized to act on behalf of owner with respect to this agreement, to manage the premises, and is owner's duly designated agent for service of process with respect to any matter arising under this agreement.

18. **HOLDING OVER:** This agreement may be terminated by either party at the end of the term by giving the other party thirty (30) days written notice prior to the end of the term. If no party gives such notice of intention to terminate, then this agreement will automatically be extended on a month-to-month basis with all

terms and conditions remaining in full force and effect until either party upon thirty days written notice terminates the agreement. Such notice shall become effective only on the last day of the month in which it is received. There shall be no renewal of this lease by operation of law.

19. **EVICTION:** If the rent called for under this agreement has not been received by the fifth day of the month in which it is due, then Management or its agent shall have the right to assert all legal and contractual remedies to enforce this lease and, without limitation to any other remedy, may take out a Dispossessory Warrant and have Resident, his or her family and possessions evicted from the premises. All rights and remedies available to Management by law, including but not limited to those described in this agreement, shall be cumulative and concurrent.

20. **SECURITY DEPOSIT:** The aforementioned security deposit will be returned to resident within thirty days after dwelling is vacated IF: a) lease term has expired or agreement has been terminated by all parties, and b) all monies due Management by Resident have been paid, and c) dwelling is not damaged beyond normal wear and tear, and d) dwelling is returned in clean, ready-to-rent condition.

21. **EARLY TERMINATION:** Resident may terminate this agreement prior to previously stated TERMINATION DATE by doing all of the following: a) Giving Management sixty days written notice, with such notice becoming effective on the last day of the month in which it is received, b) Paying all monies due through new date of termination, c) Paying an amount equal to the Security Deposit as an Early Termination Fee, d) Returning dwelling in a clean, ready-to-rent condition, and e) Paying a pro-rated portion of expenses for repainting and cleaning based on the ratio of the number of months then remaining in the initial term to the number of months originally in the initial term.

22. **APPLIANCES:** The stove, refrigerator, and window air conditioners,

and/or any other appliances, if any, delivered with the premises are for the convenience of the Resident, but are not guaranteed to operate for the duration of this agreement. If resident makes use of these items, Resident agrees to be responsible for any needed repairs to said appliances, and to return same at end of lease in same condition as at beginning of lease. Items of personality delivered with the premises are listed previously as "Appliances."

23. **REPAIRS:** Management will make necessary repairs to the dwelling and systems including electrical, plumbing, heating and hot water heating with reasonable promptness after receipt of written notice from resident. Resident agrees to bear the first $50.00 of the cost of these repairs during each calendar month. Management will bear all costs above the first $50.00 for repairs. If any damage, beyond normal wear and tear, is caused by resident or his guest, resident agrees to pay management the cost of repair with the next rent payment or upon termination of this agreement, whichever comes first. During the term of this agreement, Resident agrees to notify Management of any circumstance or condition which might cause damage to premises or which might threaten the health or safety of any person. Resident shall not remodel or make structural changes to the premises without written approval of Management.

24. **FROZEN OR BROKEN WATER PIPES:** During cool weather, Resident agrees to maintain sufficient heat in dwelling and leave faucets dripping to prevent frozen or broken water pipes.

25. **MAIL:** Mail delivery to the premises is not guaranteed, and any boxes requested by the U.S. Postal Service are not the responsibility of Management.

26. **RENTER'S INSURANCE:** Resident shall provide insurance for Resident's personal belongings in an amount satisfactory to Resident. Management shall not be liable for any damage to Resident's property, unless such damage is caused by Management's gross negligence. Resident, for himself and his family, hereby

waives all exemptions or benefits under the homestead laws of the state in which the premises are located.

27. **KEROSENE HEATERS OR APPLIANCES:** The Resident agrees not to use any form of Kerosene space heater in the dwelling.

28. **TELEPHONES:** Availability of telephone service, satellite or cable television service, or any other service to the premises is not guaranteed, and any installation or repair charges are the sole responsibility of the Resident. Installation of any such service at the premises shall occur only with the written approval of Management, and any damages to the premises as a result of such installation, including, but not limited to, holes in the walls and floors, shall be the responsibility of resident and shall not be considered normal wear and tear.

29. **SMOKE DETECTORS:** The Resident acknowledges the presence of a working smoke detector on each level of the premises, and agrees to test the detector(s) weekly for proper operation, and further agrees to replace batteries when necessary. Resident agrees to notify Management immediately in writing if any unit fails to operate properly during any test. Resident acknowledges that he understands how to test and operate the smoke detector(s) in this dwelling.

30. **LOCKS:** Resident is prohibited from adding locks to, changing or in any way altering locks installed on the doors on the premises without the prior written consent of the management. If the addition or changing of such locks is consented to, the Resident shall promptly provide management with keys to such locks.

31. **NO ESTATE IN LAND:** This lease shall create the relationship of landlord and tenant between management and resident; no estate shall pass out of the management; resident has only a usufruct and not an estate for years.

32. **SEVERABILITY:** In the event that any part of this lease be construed as unenforceable, the remaining parts of this lease shall

be in full force and effect as though the unenforceable part or parts were not written into this lease.

33. **PEST CONTROL:** Pest control is the responsibility of the resident.

34. **GENDER AND HEADINGS:** In all references herein to Resident, the use of the singular number is intended to include the appropriate number as the text of this lease may require. Each Resident shall always be jointly and severally liable for the performance of every agreement and promise made herein. Headings in this agreement are used only for convenience and ease of reference and are not to be considered in the construction or interpretation of nay provision of the agreement.

35. **LEGAL DESCRIPTION:** The full legal description of the said Premises is the same as is recorded with the Clerk of the Superior Court of the County in which the Premises is located and is made a part of this agreement by reference.

In Witness Whereof, the parties hereto have caused these presents to be signed in person or by a person duly authorized, the day and year above written. Within three business days after the date of the termination of occupancy, Management shall inspect the premises and compile a comprehensive list of any damage done to the premises and the estimated dollar value of such damage. The Resident shall have the right to inspect the premises within five business days after the termination of occupancy in order to ascertain the accuracy of the list. If the Resident refuses to sign the list, he shall state specifically in writing the items on the list to which he dissents and shall sign such statement of dissent, which must then be presented to management.

_____
MANAGEMENT   Date

_____
RESIDENT(S)   Date

Note: It is recommended that you locate a state-specific lease. You can purchase a ready-to-complete lease from most office supply stores. (This lease is pretty extensive and designed to include everything possible. Remember it is better to have too much than not enough.)

APPENDIX: 17

Move-in checklist

Landlord-Tenant Checklist

GENERAL CONDITION OF RENTAL UNIT AND PREMISES

Street Address   Unit Number   City

	Condition on Arrival	Condition on Departure	Estimated Cost of Repair/Replacement
LIVING ROOM			
Floors & Floor Coverings			
Drapes & Window Coverings			
Walls & Ceilings			
Light Fixtures			
Windows, Screens & Doors			
Front Door & Locks			
Fireplace			
Other			
Other			
KITCHEN			
Floors & Floor Coverings			
Walls & Ceilings			
Light Fixtures			
Cabinets			
Counters			
Stove/Oven			
Refrigerator			
Dishwasher			
Garbage Disposal			
Sink & Plumbing			
Windows, Screens & Doors			
Other			
Other			
DINING ROOM			
Floors & Floor Covering			
Walls & Ceilings			

	Condition on Arrival	Condition on Departure	Estimated Cost of Repair/Replacement
Light Fixtures			
Windows, Screens & Doors			
Other			
BATHROOM(S)	**Bath 1 Bath 2**	**Bath 1 Bath 2**	
Floors & Floor Coverings			
Walls & Ceilings			
Windows, Screens & Doors			
Light Fixtures			
Bathtub/Shower			
Sink & Counters			
Toilet			
Other			
Other			
BEDROOM(S)	**Bdrm 1 Bdrm 2 Bdrm 3**	**Bdrm 1 Bdrm 2 Bdrm 3**	
Floors & Floor Coverings			
Windows, Screens & Doors			
Walls & Ceilings			
Light Fixtures			
Other			
Other			
Other			
Other			
OTHER AREAS			
Heating System			
Air Conditioning			
Lawn/Garden			
Stairs and Hallway			
Patio, Terrace, Deck, etc.			
Basement			
Parking Area			
Other			
Other			
Other			
Other			
Other			

❏ Tenants acknowledge that all smoke detectors and fire extinguishers were tested in their presence and found to be in working order, and that the testing procedure was explained to them. Tenants agree to test all detectors at least once a month and to report any problems to Landlord/Manager in writing.

Tenants agree to replace all smoke detector batteries as necessary.

FURNISHED PROPERTY

	Condition on Arrival	Condition on Departure	Estimated Cost of Repair/Replacement
LIVING ROOM			
Coffee Table			
End Tables			
Lamps			
Chairs			
Sofa			
Other			
Other			
KITCHEN			
Broiler Pan			
Ice Trays			
Other			
Other			
DINING AREA			
Chairs			
Stools			
Table			
Other			
Other			
BATHROOM(S)	Bath 1 Bath 2	Bath 1 Bath 2	
Mirrors			
Shower Curtain			
Hamper			
Other			
BEDROOM(S)	Bdrm 1 Bdrm 2 Bdrm 3	Bdrm 1 Bdrm 2 Bdrm 3	
Beds (single)			
Beds (double)			
Chairs			
Chests			
Dressing Tables			
Lamps			
Mirrors			
Night Tables			
Other			

	Condition on Arrival	Condition on Departure	Estimated Cost of Repair/Replacement
Other			
OTHER AREAS			
Bookcases			
Desks			
Pictures			
Other			
Other			

Use this space to provide any additional explanation:

_____
_____
_____
_____
_____
_____
_____
_____
_____
_____
_____
_____

Landlord-Tenant Checklist completed on moving in on _____, and approved by:

_____   _____
Landlord/Manager   and   Tenant

                                          _____
                                          Tenant

                                          _____
                                          Tenant

Landlord-Tenant Checklist completed on moving out on _____, and approved by:

_____   _____
Landlord/Manager   and   Tenant

                                          _____
                                          Tenant

                                          _____
                                          Tenant

APPENDIX: 18

Tracking Form

PROPERTY ADDRESS
1000 HIGHLAND AVENUE, ANYWHERE US 10000

Outflows	JAN	FEB	MAR	APR	MAY	JUN	JULY	AUG	SEPT	OCT	NOV	DEC	Y-T-D
Mortgage Payments	750	750	750	750	750	750	750	750	750	750	750	750	9000
Advertising													
Taxes	incl	incl	incl	incl	incl	incl	incl	Incl	incl	incl	incl	incl	
Insurance	incl	incl	incl	incl	incl	incl	incl	Incl	incl	incl	incl	incl	
Management Fee	47	47	47	47	47	47	47	47	47	47	47	47	564
Utilities													
Maintenance & Repairs						90						50	140
Lawn	20												20
Misc.													
Total Outflow	817	797	797	797	797	835	797	797	797	797	797	847	9100
Rental Payments	950	950	950	950	950	950	950	950	950	950	950	950	11400
Refunds													
Other													
Total Inflow	950	950	950	950	950	950	950	950	950	950	950	950	11400
Profit	133	153	153	153	153	115	153	153	153	153	153	103	1728
Notes:													
*Receipts attached	$20					$90						$50	

Used for Rental property tracking

Based on 5% Management fee

Usually will not incur advertising charges unless you are managing the property yourself. Lawn in most cases is tenant responsibility, may have to incur until property is rented.

If you are managing property yourself, should keep rental deposits separate (some states require that deposits are held in an interest bearing bank account. Be sure to read the Landlord book of laws for your state)

For simplicity when you set up your Limited Liability Company bank account, set up a savings account as well to keep deposits, have all deposits made out to your LLC.

At the end of the year, you will readily be able to see your total outflow, inflow, expenses and net profit for the property.

It is also a good idea to take your mortgage statement and breakdown, how much of the payment is principal and how much is interest. The amount of interest that is paid is tax deductible; you will also receive an interest statement tax form at the end of the year from each mortgage company.

APPENDIX: 19

Net worth calculation

It is important that while you are building your wealth you understand your net worth position at all times. In this Appendix is a completed net worth worksheet reflecting the real estate holdings from our plan. After all, you should definitely know how much you are worth!

Net-Worth Calculation Worksheet

An important step in gaining financial control is to calculate your net worth (assets - debts). Every year, your net worth should be tabulated to review your progress and compare it with your financial goals. In addition, a net-worth statement is a valuable aid in planning your estate and establishing a record for loan and insurance purposes.

Assets (What You Own)

Cash:

Cash On Hand _____

Checking Account _____

Savings Accounts _____

Money Market Funds _____

Cash Value of Life Insurance _____

Other _____

Real Estate/Property:

Home _____

Land _____

Other _____

Investments: (*Market Value*)

Certificates of Deposit _____

Stocks _____

Bonds _____

Mutual Funds _____

Annuities _____

IRAs _____

401(k),403(b), 457 Plans _____

Pension Plan _____

Other _____

Personal Property: (*Present Value*)

Automobiles _____

Recreational Vehicle/Boat _____

Home Furnishings _____

Appliances and Furniture _____

Collections _____

Jewelry and Furs _____

Other _____

Total Assets _____

Liabilities (What You Owe)

Current Debts:

Household _____

Medical _____

Credit Cards _____

Department Store Cards _____

Back Taxes _____

Legal _____

Other _____

Mortgages:

Home _____

Land _____

Other _____

Loans:

Bank/Finance Company _____

Bank/Finance Company _____

Automobile _____

Recreational Vehicle/Boat _____

Education _____

Life Insurance _____

Personal (from family or friends) _____

Other _____

Total Liabilities _____

Total Assets Minus Total Liabilities = Net Worth _____

NOTES

About the author

Wealth builder, educator, author and speaker, Sonia Booker is one of the nation's leading "Go To" wealth experts. Entrepreneur, author, inspirational speaker and real estate guru, Sonia's niche is helping people move from everyday living to wealth building. She is an award winning author of the bestseller **Real Estate and Wealth:** *Investing in the American Dream*, writing this book to provide a simple, step-by step guide to purchasing real estate as an investment to build your wealth. Sonia's anticipated follow up book **Real Estate and Wealth:** *Investing in the American Dream: The New Edition* again takes a basic approach and encourages everyone to get started building wealth no matter where you are in life.

From owning an Allstate Insurance agency at the age of 24, Sonia began using her profits from this business to purchase investment property quickly discovering her passion for real estate. She soon sold her agency to invest in real estate full time. Sonia has carved out a unique position for herself in the marketplace through her down-to-earth approach and by going through what she considers to be the school of hard knocks. Her knowledge and business experience enables her to continuously inform, inspire and engage others to define and enjoy wealth for themselves.

She first captured national attention when she appeared in Black Enterprise 2002, showing off one of her renovation projects. Two years later she wrote her first book on real estate investing after putting together the steps to success in a self-published book, which later caught the eye of Amber Publishing becoming an Essence Bestseller.

Sonia has graced the covers of numerous magazines including, Onyx Woman, Average Girl and is often sought after for speaking engagements, radio and TV interviews appearing on Fox 5 providing real estate tips. You can catch Sonia on many of the top business shows or speaking at a number of national business conferences.

She is a regular presenter for Home Buyer Conferences, National Urban League, National Black MBA Association, and George Fraser's PowerNetworking Conference. She has also appeared in Upscale, Atlanta Voice, Booking Matters and Rolling Out.

Sonia grew up around real estate and entrepreneurs, it is no wonder, this Jackson, MS native, Atlanta implant feels right at home purchasing real estate and sharing her knowledge of success through investing. Since 2006, Sonia has worked with her mentor and friend Herman J. Russell (H.J. Russell & Company) who founded one of the largest real estate construction and management companies in the southeast. She has partnered and worked hand-in-hand on condo conversion projects, hotels and other commercial properties.

Sonia is passionate about the advancement of women and founded the Inner Circle Women's Investor Association, a group of progressive women who share a common interest of building wealth and leaving a legacy. As a wife and mother, she understands the demands of women and the multi-tasking required to positively impact the family. Sonia has served on the board of the YWCA of Metro Atlanta and Chayil, Inc. (Domestic Violence Recovery) and City of Hope. "I love to impact the lives of others especially women. Once I am on your side and believe in your mission I am just there helping however I can. I give generously of my time and money to help make an impact."

Sonia is a long-standing member of the Ray of Hope Church and has a wonderful spiritual relationship with her pastor, Dr. Cynthia Hale.

About Herman J. Russell, Sr.

Born into a blue-collar family in the Jim Crow South, Herman J. Russell built a shoeshine business when he was twelve years old and used the profits to buy a vacant lot where he built a duplex while he was still a teen. Over the next fifty years, he continued to build businesses, amassing on the nation's most profitable minority owned conglomerates.

The H.J. Russell &Company is a diversified organization, headquarters in Atlanta and operates in the areas of construction, construction management, real estate development and property management. In addition, Mr. Russell's business interest have also grown to include Concessions International, LLC, with food and beverage units in several major airports, and ownership in Paschal's restaurant, which is a cornerstone in his Castleberry Hill development, which has revitalized the southwest edge of downtown Atlanta. Today, Herman Russell is the chairman of his enterprises, which generate revenues of over $300 million dollars, and ensure jobs for 2,500 employees and affordable homes for thousands of people.

From the time of his beginning during the turbulent years of the early civil rights movement, Herman J. Russell has built one of the greatest success stories in America and is a role model for African-American entrepreneurship. He has left a lasting impression on the communities, which he has worked, with some of the nations most celebrated skylines bearing his imprint. The most significant evidence of his corporate portfolio can be seen in his hometown of Atlanta, and includes work with major Fortune 500 companies such as Georgia Pacific, Delta Airlines and the Coca-Cola Company, as well as Turner Field and the Georgia World Congress Center and the soon to be built Falcons Stadium.

Mr. Russell is a philanthropist, giving back to his community with generosity. He believes strongly that the youth of today need strong positive role models and mentors. To that end, he founded the Herman J. Russell Foundation, Inc., which is focused on stimulating the self-sufficiency of youth and the community in which they live.

He is a graduate of Tuskegee University and the celebrated author of *Building Atlanta*, a book where he shares his inspiring life story and reveals how he overcame racism, poverty, and a debilitation speech impediment to become one of the most successful African American entrepreneurs, Atlanta civic leaders, and unsung heroes of the civil rights movement.

NOTES

Made in the USA
Columbia, SC
07 March 2024